MISGUIDED LOVE
Memoirs of a Teenaged Sex Addict

Kevin L. Sanders

iUniverse, Inc.
New York   Bloomington

iUniverse books may be ordered through booksellers or by contacting:

iUniverse
1663 Liberty Drive
Bloomington, IN 47403
www.iuniverse.com
1-800-Authors (1-800-288-4677)

ISBN: 978-1-4401-1639-1 (sc)
ISBN: 978-1-4401-1640-7 (ebook)

Printed in the United States of America

iUniverse rev. date: 02/04/2009

This book is dedicated
To the memory of the beautiful Ms. Ruby L. Sanders
My heart and soul… I love you always.
(Thanks Mama)

Contents

Chapter 1

Family Values

TALL, DARK AND HANDSOME. That was me. Eric Monroe. I was a B-average student at C. Anderson high school in Charleston, South Carolina. I was a simple kid I suppose. Never got into trouble or hung with the wrong crowd. Y'see my Mama raised me right. My parents divorced when I was nine years old. My Dad didn't spend much time with me after that. My most vivid remembrance was of him showing me porno movies when I was about seven years old. I had no idea that that's what people did when kids weren't around! That was nasty. I couldn't help watching though. It fascinated me. I remember the smell of liquor on his breath as he passed on the fatherly advice to me… "Don't ever tell your Mama I showed you this… don't be no faggot boy… make your Daddy proud".

He didn't have to worry about me saying anything to Mama. Maaaan… my Mama would'a killed me …*and* him! Dad packed my head full with images of naked women and people doing it so much that I was drawing pictures of it in school! I couldn't explain to the Principal where I learned that stuff, because everybody knew my Mama didn't play that mess! As I got older, Dad's visits got fewer. I guess he felt he raised me well enough and I would be just fine. Some of my friends never even met their Dad's so I guess I was lucky. That was all right though, because I knew one day I was going to be a famous architect. I loved to build things. I remember my first leggo set. I built a city. I made a blueprint when I was ten years old of the house I was gonna build for Mama. I kept it under my bed. Dad thought that career was unrealistic for me. I'd show him. I'd do it just for my Mama. She was my best friend. We went through it all together. From government cheese to yard sales, we did it all. It all brought us closer. I loved her and she loved me. Nothing ever came between us. Well, at least up until my senior year. I remember when I got my car! It was the summer of 1988 and in two months I would be a senior in high school. It was hot out and my flat top was growing crooked! Worse than that…I had no ride! I just couldn't start my senior year off walking! I had to wait for the perfect time to spring it on Ma. I caught her while she was on the phone with Grandma.

"Yo Ma, can I get a car?" I asked.

"Hold on a second Mama," she said annoyed. "This boy obviously doesn't see me on the phone. Yo Eric, get a job this summer and we'll talk about it."

"Yes!" I exclaimed, as I jumped on her and kissed her. "Get off me boy!" Mama laughed.

I got a job at Burger King and began saving every penny. Finally, at the end of the summer I had about $600.00. I would've had more, but I had to help Ma with some of the bills. That was cool though, because a week before school started, we went out and got me a 1987 Nissan Stanza. Black. Ma paid for the initials and stuff and I was on the road! Man, I loved that car. I washed it almost every day. Even in the rain! Yeah baby. I was startin'my senior year off right!

First day of school. A senior. Finally, the underclass students would look up to me. Aw yeah! It always seemed like schools smelled funny on the first day. All the fellas looked the same, give or take a few inches of hair. However, some of the girls were lookin' *right*! They must've beauty-slept all summer! I tried to get some of their phone numbers but none of my classmen took me seriously or gave me any play because A: I wasn't popular; B: I wasn't *light-skinned*; and C: I definitely didn't have any money. So I took what I could get. I hated it though. I couldn't understand why you had to settle because of what's on your outside. Who wrote that rule? It's a good thing momz always told me to accept myself for what I was because "God don't make no mistakes." Everybody was wearing their new clothes. I had on my one and only red Polo shirt. It was all I could afford as far as the cool clothes went. I had the fresh two-toned Levi's on me. I even got a few looks. Little did they know that I would rock them same jeans for the majority of the school year. Gotta make do. That was how it was. I didn't have an older brother and I still wore hand me downs! Saturday mornings my Mama was up and out to every Yard Sale that was out. That's how I got my gear. Funny thing was when my crew would be like, "Yo Eric, where'd you get this or that?" I'd be like…

"Oh this old mess? Man… I think it came from the mall or something."

Lying my butt off! I bet they Mamas were doing the same thing on Saturdays. They probably would be laughing at the clothes they were getting us. It was cool though because I was in school to learn. I dang sho' won't there for no girls. Mama said that as smart as I was, I didn't have to worry about that. It would happen when I was ready.

My classes were so-so, and my lunch hour was so-so. After the first week, the routine became tedious. Being a senior had to be more than this. I mean, after two weeks, all I'd gotten was off-campus lunch, a school parking space, and hall privileges. Big freakin' deal!

"Word! That's what I'm sayin' man." my homie Tyrone said. "I mean, I was thinkin' we could do all kinds of crazy stuff! Like skip classes, smack the teachers, and get laid everyday!"

Tyrone was a nut! We had known each other since the second grade. He hadn't changed since then!

"Yo man, did you see DiSonne Curtis? Tyrone asked. "Damn she fine! When she walks by, her butt be callin' me."

"Say what?"

"No seriously man." he continued. "The other day she walked by me right?"

"Right."

"So I hear this voice saying, *Tyrone… Tyrone… over here.*" Then when I look, that booty be right in my face! Yo, mark my words man, I'ma get them panties before we graduate."

"Right Tyrone."

"You just watch me boy." he assured himself.

"Man the only thing you're gonna get is blisters on the inside of your hands from chokin' yo' chicken!"

"Man-n-n-n, forget you Eric. *Your* virgin ass aint gettin' no booty."

"Crazy? I'm gettin' it everyday bo-e-e-y!"

He knew I was lying, so instead of continuing the argument he simply said,

"Sheeee….."

That was his trademark expression. If it was outside of his realm of reality, you could count on hearing that.

A month of school had passed, and I was doing rather well. I decided to help Ma out more with the bills. She didn't even ask me. I would even cook dinner for her when she would come home from work. I loved Mama. I was so proud of her. When Dad left, she never got with any other man. She always told me she didn't need any other man. She said that God would help her raise me. She was always so proud of me. Oh how she'd brag to the neighbors about me.

"My baby's gonna be a famous architect one day, so he can build his Mama her own house."

Yeah, I wanted to be an architect. I just love constructing pieces to make a whole (so to speak). I can even remember when I got my first Lego set. I tried to build an entire city! Building fascinated me. Ma didn't know it but I *did* plan to build her that dream house.

I loved my Mama.

She was my best friend. We were always close because we went through so much together. I guess when you suffer with someone, you really grow closer. I remembered one summer we went through together. Dad was hardly givin' us any money. We started getting food stamps and stuff. I hated when Ma would take me to the store with those things! It was so un-cool. Especially if a fly girl was on the register. Ma used to say…

"That's alright baby. Mamas gonna go get *her* some food to eat tonight. You just stay here and be cool."

Most kids my age weren't close with their folks. Not me though. *Mommycakes* was my girl. She taught me everything I knew. From manners to math. I knew I could always go to her for anything. For any answer. We discussed everything. Except for sex. That was always the unspoken subject in the house. I guess Ma never looked at me like I could do anything like that. The one and only time it came up, the look of fear on her face let me know not to ever bring it up again. Well, Dad didn't teach me anything. Unless you counted his dirty magazines and his porno tapes.

I was at lunch off-campus one day when who do I run into? Tisha, my baby cousin! Now Tish' was my girl, with her crazy self. We used to hang out all the time. She was in the 11th grade so……..

"Wait a minute," I said. "What are you doing off-campus girl? You aint no senior!"

"Yeah, I know", she replied "but I got it like that!"

I gave her our customary big ole' teddy-bear hug. I loved my cousin Tisha, with her worrisome self. As we sat, she told me that she wanted to go out that night. Since it was a Friday and I was off work, I was down. So that night I let Ma know that I was going out with Tisha. She said her usual 'Be careful baby.' Ma said that every time I got ready to go somewhere. I wondered why? Oh well. When I got to Tisha's house, I said 'what up' to Aunt Jean. Uncle Pete was still working at the chemical plant, downtown. He worked all kinds of crazy hours.

"Hello Eric." Aunt Jean said as dry as she could. She was a trip. She would look at you as though she could see right through you. Man, I bet Uncle Pete was paranoid as hell! Tisha finally came out of her room and said bye to Aunt Jean.

"Don't worry Aunt Jean, I'll keep her out of trouble." I said with a chuckle, trying to cut the tension. She looked right past me and said "12 o'clock Tisha."

"Yes Mam." she replied.

Man, we got out of that house quick-like! As soon as we got in the car Tisha goes,

"Oh yeah, we gotta pick up some folk!"

I knew she would come with some last minute jive. I hated when she did that. I mean, I feel like this, tell me everything from the jump. Don't pull that surprise act on me. I should've cussed her out, but she's my baby cuz. So once again I let her get over. Crazy girl. She directs me to this dude she's supposed to be seeing's house. She jumps out to go get this guy. Meanwhile, I'm in the car about to dookie on myself because this dude's neighborhood was jacked up! One street light for three blocks. I had to leave my headlights on just to see! Bums all up and down the street. I was praying that none of them would ask me for money. The houses looked like they were made of straw. The store on the corner's lights kept blinking on and off. And I was sittin' out there counting how many rats I saw with knives!

"Aw man, where the hell was Tisha?" I thought.

I was gonna kick her ass for this one! Not that I minded coming to certain hoods, I'd just like to know in advance so I could pack my bat in the trunk. Now that was messed up that I was scared to be in a black neighborhood. Especially being black. Five minutes later, she came strolling out of the house with this little muscle-bound pimp.

"Eric, this is James. James, this is my cousin Eric." she said happily.

I looked at her like Aunt Jean had looked at me. When they got in I whispered in Tisha's ear.

"If-this-night-doesn't-pick-up--you're dead meat!"

"Oh it will cuz, don't worry. Now we gotta pick up my other homie."

I knew it! So after driving around town for half an hour, we finally get to this big red house. Tisha jumps out of the car as usual, and goes to ring the doorbell. I waited to see if another *Arnold Schwartza-midget* would come out. If he did, I'd probably kick this guy out and leave all three of them. I was just about to honk my horn when this fly-girl came out! She had on this orange shirt with these black jeans and black sneakers. I'd seen her before, but I couldn't remember where. Damn, she was fly!

I couldn't wait for an intro... and Tisha knew it. That's why she didn't say anything when they got in the car. Tisha could read me like a book.

After a few moments, the silence was broken when Tisha said,

"Oh yeah Eric, this is Yolana."

Ya -what? I thought. Nevertheless, I had to play it cool, so I said,

"What up?"

She responded from behind my seat with,

"Hi!"

She sounded like Punky Brewster or somebody, but it didn't faze me. We went to this club called the Tunnel. It was packed as usual. 'Round my way, folk came out the house for few reasons. To catch a sale, or to party. It was kickin' inside! We basically walked around and stuff. Then the DJ put on "I Like" from GUY. Oh smack! Now that was my song! I asked Tish' to dance with me so I could wax her as usual.

"Why don't you ask Yolana? She's over there waiting for you to ask her."

I didn't even hesitate. I just walked right over and....

"Excuse me. You wanna dance?"

"Yep."

Cool. I couldn't believe I did that. Man I was gettin' rather bold!

I could tell she was a woman of few words, so I took her by the hand and led her to the dancefloor. We jammed! I was doing my best M.C. Hammer impersonation, while she was shakin' her thang left and right. We were on the floor for at least an hour straight. She was pretty cool. We could've danced all night, but we all had to leave because some fools started fighting and somebody pulled a gun. I couldn't tell if who it was, because we were gone like the 1950's.

"Man I wish some Negroes would just wake the hell up and stop fightin' each other. Damn! You don't see white folk doin' that stupidity. That's why we can't have nothin'. And that's why the cops think we're *all* criminals. I mean, why would you bring a gun to a club? Who are you, security?"

I didn't realize it, but I was talking a mile a minute. I didn't care though because that kind of stuff irked me.

"Now where to?" I asked, figuring Tisha had the whole night planned out.

"Let's go to the playground behind Powell." she said. Powell was my old Elementary school. Bet. When we pulled into the school's driveway, I dimmed my lights because of the residential area. When we all got out, Tisha grabbed James and mumbled,

"Excuse us."

That left me alone with Yolana. When I turned to look at her, she was smiling at me. So after a few moments of silence, I tried to break the ice.

"Y'know, if you keep practicing, one day you'll be able to hang with me on the dance floor."

She laughed, and we started walking.

"So whose idea was it to name you Yolana?"

"My Mama's."

"What does it mean?"

"Huh?"

"Does it have some type of African meaning?" I asked stupidly.

"Not that I know of." she responded with a chuckle.

She asked if I was a senior, so I pointed to my chin.

"You see these beard hairs don't you?"

"Very funny."

She said she was in the tenth grade. I was sort of disappointed, but it was all right. Her body was so developed, it had already graduated! We sat down by the parallel bars. Tish' and what's his name came by. Tisha mumbled something to the effect of "Go ahead boy!" Words of encouragement I took. When they passed, I looked at Yolana and boldly asked,

"Do you have a boyfriend?"

"Nope."

(Yes!)

"Do you have a girlfriend?"

"If I did, you wouldn't be here shorty."

She smiled. I was a little nervous but I was going for broke. I saw that she was nervous too, so I extended my arms towards her and whispered,

"Come here."

We both knew what that meant. We kissed. It's something about kissing someone for the first time. It almost tingles. I liked that. I patted my lap and told her to have a seat. She stood and straddled my hips. We wrapped our arms around each other. I looked into her eyes. I couldn't think of a movie-line or anything, so I just said,

"You know I like you, don't you?"

"I like you too Eric. I like you a lot."

(Aw, shucks!)

I had her wrapped by this point, so I played that role.

"Oh you do? How much?"

She came in close and whispered in my ear.

"If we were alone, I'd show you how much."

(Aw, hell!)

I'd never heard a female come off all direct like that before! I was shocked, yet somewhat aroused. We started kissing again, this time we tongued. We were gettin' into the groove when..... here came Tisha.

"Well it's about damn time!" she exclaimed.

On the way back, Tisha and what's his face, wanted to ride in the backseat. It was cool with me, because Yolana got to sit in the front seat with me. We took James home first, and waited five minutes for Tisha to take her tongue out of his mouth. When she got back to the car, she and Yolana did some hi-five with a fingersnap. Girls. So dramatic. I was putting in my new TROOP tape when I saw the time on my clock radio. That mob said 11:48p.m.! I had to do a double take 'cause I knew Tisha curfew was at 12:00a.m. If she came in at 12:01, that would've been the end of her butt. I knew Aunt Jean didn't play!

"Yo Tish'?" I called as calmly as possible.

"What?"

"Look what time it is."

When she saw my clock, her smile dropped. Then we all said, "Oh snap!"

I hit the gas so fast, the paint almost came off my car! Tisha was in the backseat thinkin' up excuses. I was too, because I knew Aunt Jean would call Ma and even *make up* some stuff on me! The time was 11:56p.m. I turned down Tilmore drive, which was the street they lived on, but they lived all the way down at the end. I was doin' 60mph down that 35mph drive. I didn't care. The cops weren't nothing compared to Aunt Jean. Man she's the closest to the military I ever wanted to get! I yelled back to Tisha,

"Yo, we almost there. When I turn into the driveway, Yolana'll open your door. Girl, you betta' dive out like yo' ass is one of the Dukes of Hazard!"

We did just that. Their porch light was on as usual and Tisha made it in at 11:59p.m.

Their porch light was timed to go off at exactly 12:00 a.m. That's how I knew she made it. Man, it was like boot camp over their house. I bet Aunt Jean was standing' right behind the door with a frying pan! I'm glad my mom wasn't like that. I would've been dead by then, and that's for sure. Then I realized..... I was alone with Yolana.

"Now what time is your curfew?" I asked.

"I don't have one."

"Yeah right, you're in the tenth grade and you don't have a curfew."

"That's right."

I didn't retaliate because I wanted to spend more time with her. I wanted to kiss her again. I didn't want to force it though, so I asked her where her house was.

"I don't feel like going home, Eric."

Feeling my collar tighten, I asked,

"What do you feel like doing then?"

"Let's go somewhere."

I didn't even ask where, I just started driving. I took her to the back of this old furniture store. It was completely deserted. Without much talk, we went at it. As my tongue tasted hers, my hands instinctively went to her tits, and they felt good!

She reached over and squeezed my joint through my jeans. Either she was shocked by my size or just trying to blow my ego up when she said, "Boy, you big!"

I kissed her harder. I unbuttoned her shirt and gazed at the curves around her purple bra. I lifted the cup and started licking her nipples. I sucked liked I wanted milk. She put her hand on the back of my head and moaned, "Eric." That just made me hornier. So with my free hand, smooth-like, I slid down between her legs. It was like a furnace down there. I'm surprised her jeans didn't ignite! I was so psyched. I was ready to do her. Just then I remembered, I hadn't changed my drawers since that morning! I had played ball that afternoon before we went out. (Y'see guys don't wash as much as women do. It depends on our mood. Until then, we just carry on hoping the deodorant or the cologne will hold out.) I knew my *jones* would be stinkin' so I just stopped cold.

"What's wrong?" she asked suprised.

"Nothing."

"Don't you want me?"

"I sure do."

"I want you inside me, Eric." she whispered.

Then what does my dumb mouth say?

"Huh?"

In a clarifying tone she added, "I wanna have sex with you."

Damn, it doesn't get any more romantic than that! This stuff was blowing' my mind. I never heard a girl talk so direct. I had to come up with some excuse to decline and apologized for not finishing what I started.

"How about we get together after school tomorrow, Yolana?"

She obliged.

"By the way, I asked, what school do you go to?"

"The same school you go to Eric."

"So that's where I've seen you!" I exclaimed. She nodded her head. "Bet. I'll pick you up behind the cafeteria right after school tomorrow."

"Okay, don't front!"

"I won't Eric."

Chapter 2:

On a Platter

THE NEXT DAY IN school, I couldn't concentrate on *jack!* All I could think about was the end of the day and gettin' into Yolana's panties! All through first period I was thinking, where are we going to do this? Second period was, what position? Third, what kind of music? Fourth, what speed? Fifth, how many times? Lunch period, why not now? By the time I got to seventh period, I had figured out that we would do it in my house until it was time for Ma to come home, which was around six o'clock that evening. Eighth period I was about to burst. I didn't know where my mind was, but it sure wasn't in Chemistry class. I found myself thinking of how each and every female in class was in bed. I wanted to sex *all* of 'em. I was even thinking of my teacher, Mrs. McCally's old rusty butt. I was so horny I could've done a goat!

"Isn't that correct, Eric?" I heard Mrs. McCally say with extreme sarcasm.

(Dang! Busted.)

"Just what are you thinking about young man?"

("Your old wrinkled booty!")

She-e-i-i-t, I wish I would've said something like that.

"I'm sorry Mrs. McCally, I've just got a lot of things on my mind."

"Well, if the **things on your mind** are not about Chemistry, then I suggest you keep them out of my classroom!"

The whole class laughed at me. At least I didn't get detention-hall.

The final bell rang. I think I made it to my car before the other students even hit the hallway. When I got in my car I started wiping the sweat off my face and checking for my armpits. Cool, I was ready. I drove to the back of the cafeteria. Naturally, I got there before she did.

After about three minutes I started getting nervous. Then finally, here she comes, bouncing up the sidewalk.

"Sorry I'm late," she said. "I had to go to my locker."

"Are you ready?"

"Yeah."

"Cool, let's go."

We sped off. When we got to the crib, I gave her a thirty second tour of the house. Then, it was off to my room. She said she liked the way my room looked. "Thanks", I said. That's about all it took until clothes started comin' off! Her shirt, my pants, her shorts, my necklace, her bra, my watch, her panties. By the time she was fully naked, I was still in my shirt and drawers, (clean ones that time!). She laid down on my bed and blew a kiss to me. I just stood there, stiff as a mummy. I wasn't a virgin or nothin'. Well, I had done it before. Once. Yucky experience. When I was 14, this guy we called "Black-Rat", and I got this girl from his old neighborhood in the apartment's laundry room. I didn't know where I was or what I was doing. I was in way over my head. She was older than we were…dumber too. She pulled her pants down, sat on the washing machine, and told me to stick it in. All I knew about sex was what I saw in my Dad's dirty books. So I stuck it in. I tried to kiss her like in the movies, but she didn't want to kiss me. She kept turning her face away as she pulled me back and forward in her. After about five minutes, she told me to take it out so she could do it with Black-Rat. I hated it. I hated her. I was so sick, that I had to go outside. Anyway, I thought, "When I get through with Yolana, she'll think I'm a pro!" I started looking for my rubbers. Where in the hell were they? She looked up and saw me rambling.

"It's Okay Eric, I'm on the pill."

Suddenly, I could hear my Dad's voice when he used to say, "Don't ever trust a woman when she says that." I heard her sigh. On top of that, I was goin' limp. Besides, I could always pull out before I came. I laid on the bed next to her and slid between her legs. Since I was little soft, I had to reach down and guide him in. Her walls were hot as hell! It felt like my stuff was being broiled! I got harder by the second. She exploded within minutes. Then she started screaming my name.

"Eric.., oh Eric!"

I felt like Superman then. I was just about to get into the groove when...... oh hell naw. Hell naw man! Damn!! I felt myself coming too soon so I pulled out and started fondling her. I knew what was coming next.

"Is something wrong, Eric?"

(Yeah, I can't control my stuff.). A few minutes later, I got hard again. I screwed her brains out! For the next few weeks, we kept meeting, and kept doing it. I loved it. It got so familiar, that I started coming in her. She never mentioned pregnancy or a deep relationship, so as far as I was concerned, I had my own private *booty.*

Then there was Sheila. Sheila was my supervisor at my part-time home, Burger King. She was a twenty-two year old college senior who majored in criminal law. I tried to rap to her and two of her girlfriends all last summer, but they all dissed me. Anna, who was twenty-four, said I had no chance in hell with her because I was a growing boy, and she was not my priority. Tammy, twenty-three, said I was just too young period. Sheila basically came off the same. I mean, it wasn't that they were that fine, it was just that they were there.

After school one day, I was out playing b-ball with Tyrone and the guys. I liked playing basketball. I didn't want it for a career though. Too many brothers shot for that goal. Then when they don't make the cut, they wound up working in a grocery store telling legend stories for the rest of their lives. Couldn't be me.

I was winning the game, when somebody asked for the time. My watch said 4:45p.m. "Oh smack! I exclaimed. I gotta be at work by five!" I jetted. I hit the Cross-town Expressway doing at least 60mph. I'd never been late to work and I wanted people to know I took my job seriously. Eventhough all that was a crock, I still hauled "A" to get there. I finally got there at 5:07 p.m. I flew past the customers and straight to the bathroom to change. My rep was over. I could just hear Maurice, the store manager, saying, "I knew he'd be late sometime." That chump. When I went in, Maurice asked me if my stomach felt better. "Huh?" I replied.

"Sheila said you called and said you may not come in because of your stomach."

(*Cool!* Go Sheila! Get busy!) "Uh.... yes...sir, it feels a little better."

I had to thank her for the save.

"Yeah," she said. "I'm looking out for you."

"So when can I look out for you?" I said, flirting as usual.

"We'll see."

(Whaaaat?)

We sure did see too. It was the week before Thanksgiving, and we were out of school because of a teacher's workday. I decided to work that day, and guess who was working beside me? *Damn-Skippy*.......
Sheila.

I was on the carry-out register and she was bagging the food. We were working hard that day. All day I was waiting for her to give me her phone number or something.

Instead she kept right on working like she didn't say anything last week. Well I'm going for it, I thought. Just then, who do I see coming into the parking lot?

Mike. Sheila's muscle-bound, Army- reserve, prison guard boyfriend! Damn! When she spotted him, she told Tammy to fill in for her. I watched her walk all the way to him. Uh-oh! What's this? They're arguing? She must be crazy to fuss at that big mob! He's liable to get shellshock and shoot her! He handed her something that looked like money. She snatched that joint, rolled her eyes, and stormed back into the store.

"Oh brother," Tammy giggled, "here she comes!"

When she came in we were all playin' it off hard. I was looking straight up at the ceiling like I was pigeon hunting or something. Tammy was all on the floor acting like she dropped a contact lenses. Knowing she aint never wore no glasses. One dude even excused himself to go to the bathroom. When Sheila saw how everybody was actin', she smacked her lips, and rolled her eyes. Man...... I didn't say jack! After she calmed down she asked me if I had a girlfriend.

"No, I don't Sheila."

"Well when you get one, do yourself a favor and don't lie to her."

"I won't." I said. Basically because I knew that's what she wanted to hear.

"Why? Did Mike lie to you?" She rolled her eyes again. I knew she was weak, so I played my *role*. "Mike just doesn't know how lucky he is to have someone like you Sheila." She tried to thank me, but

I wouldn't let her interrupt me. "I mean, from what I know of you, you're smart, you're pretty, and.... you've got cute little teeth. There aren't that many sisters out there left with cute teeth girl." She blushed. "There, now don't you feel better?"

"Yes, thank you."

"Good, because the customers have been complaining about thumbprints in their sandwich buns!" We cracked up. "There's my smile." I said.

"Y'know you're something else Eric. Always cheering somebody up. So, what time do you get off ?"

"Yeah right, Sheila."

"I'm serious."

She *was* too. (Oh smack!)

"Three o'clock. Why?"

"Well," she said while biting her bottom lip, "I get off at two. Would you like some company later, say around four?"

"Sure!" I said, thinking Ma gets home about 5:45p.m. (YES!) I gave her my number.

"I'll call you."

"You do that." Like I had juice.

I got home at 3:20 p.m. and started cleaning like a madman. I was dusting the tables, sweeping the floor, watching videos, and scrubbing my armpits all at the same time! The phone rang at 3:30p.m. I knew it had to be Sheila, or Yolana one. I was hoping it wasn't Yolana, because I told her I wouldn't be home. Besides, she called too much. Ma hated that crap, so I told her at school that I would call her. She still called though. I answered the phone like I was hiding out from the FBI or somebody. *"Hello?"*

"Hello Eric?" It was Sheila. (Yes!)

"Hi Sheila."

"Hi, I'm at the Piggly Wiggly store. Am I near your house?"

"Yep. Just come straight down Fairfield road, and make a right at the light. It'll be the first white house you see."

"O.K. I'll be right there."

At that I ran to my room, grabbed my brush for a last minute mirror-check, and splashed on some Undeniable by Billy Dee Williams. Ma gave me that cologne for Christmas last year and until then I had no reason to use it. I could hear the air pressure when I opened it. I sprayed the house with Lysol and put on Ma's Luther Vandross album. Then I sat in the recliner like I was J.R. Ewing, just waiting for that little brown Nova of hers to pull up. What was taking so long? Please say she didn't get lost. The directions were simple! I was panicking. "Calm down Eric", I found myself saying. I went to the curtain about ten times. Finally! It had been a whole three minutes since she called! I heard her car door open and close. I couldn't believe it. Sheila was actually at my house!

"Knock Knock."

"Who is it?" I asked being cute.

"It's me, Sheila." When I opened the door, she had on a yellow v-neck sweater, spandex pants and yellow flats to match! She looked good as hell!

"Come on in."

"Thanks."

It wasn't long before we began talking about Mike. She was complaining about how she was so tired of his b.s. and all that jazz. I told her that maybe the problem with him was that he's been playin' that hard role all of his life, and that had a huge affect on why he couldn't show his soft side to her. I learned all that woman stuff from Ma. She declared that I would not turn out like my Dad. She taught me how to treat them, court them, and the whole nine yards. Just no sex. She was right too, because after about five minutes, Sheila was like putty in my hands.

"Look Sheila, you've got to live your life. So don't put it on hold for anyone."

"You sure know a lot for your age Eric." She said impressed.

"I know more than you think Sheila."

"Is that so?"

"That is so."

"Do you know how to make love to a woman?" All the while, her hand was inching up my leg.

"Is that a question or an invitation Sheila?"

She kissed me.

"What do you think?"

(A-w-w-w Shucks!)

We kissed all the way from the den to my room. I wanted her. I wanted her bad. She must've wanted me too, because by the time I reached for her top, she had unzipped my pants. We stepped away simultaneously to undress ourselves. It took me awhile because I tried to pull my pants over my sneakers! When I looked back up, my mouth almost hit the floor. This woman had the most gorgeous body I had ever seen! It was flawless! I mean, the women in the dirty mags Dad gave me didn't have shapes like hers. No wonder Mike tried to act so tuff. I just stood there staring. Her skin was as smooth as a Reese's peanut butter cup. I had to compliment her.

"Damn Sheila, you look good!"

She peeked down at my meat.

"Thanks, just don't hurt me with that thing."

I was about to tell her to get on the bed so I could put on my rubber. Then I thought, she's not in highschool, she probably wants me to lay her down and all that. So I did. She responded just like I thought she would. She smiled. Man, that body! I tried to slide him in like I did with Yolana. *No Haps.* So I kept trying different angles. Nothing. I had to go back down there to see if she had an opening.

"What's wrong Eric?"

Why do women say that? After ten minutes of fingering, I was back on her. When I tried to put it back in, she was still too tight. So I forced him in. After the first stroke, she screamed and dug her nails into my back. I didn't know which hurt more, her nails or her booty! She couldn't have been a virgin. Seconds later, I could feel the muscles in my legs flexing. Her stuff was squeezing me and I couldn't take it much more. So I came. I knew she was disappointed. So was I. What was my problem? I had been screwing Yolana for weeks and all was well. My conscience was buggin' the hell out of me. How could you have the perfect body on your bed, naked, and messed it up? All that time I'd been flappin' at the lip about what I would do to her and what do I do? Nut too fast. When I went back to work the next day, I was hoping not to see her. As I pulled into the parking lot, I saw her car. (Dag!) I thought she was off. Oh well, might as well get it over with. So I went on in and said my usual "what ups" to everyone. Except Sheila.

"Hi Eric." she said cheerfully.

I walked right by her as if she wasn't there. What did she mean "Hi Eric?" Like nothing happened yesterday. I clocked in and went back on line. I knew she would be working beside me. She probably scheduled it that way on purpose. For ten minutes we didn't say a word to each other. Until I reached for an order and she grabbed my hand.

"Stop it Eric." Sheila said discretely.

"What?" I said, playing dumb.

Then she gave me that threatening whisper my Mother always gave me when we were in public and she couldn't raise her voice.

"I-- said--stop--it!" She pulled me off line and put Reggie in my place. "Eric, what happened yesterday was normal." I smacked my lips. "I had a great time with you all right?" I nodded.

"But now I won't get another chance." I pouted.

"Oh yes you will." She grinned. "You don't get away that easily."

So we set another meeting for Thursday, because had to study for some exam on civil rights. I liked her being smart and all, but I bet Mike just hated that. Brothers don't like their women to be smarter than them. That's messed up. It's just like whitefolk. A lot of black men claim they love and support their black women, and they're equal. Just like some whitefolk claim they love us. But deep down inside, ignorant brothers are afraid of sisters for the same reason ignorant white people are afraid of us. They're both afraid that the other will educate and eventually overthrow them from the throne that they *think* they're on. So there's no other alternative, but to scheme. Mama taught me that too.

Thursday came quickly. I was off work after school and was waiting for my *Piggly Wiggly* call from Sheila. Ah yeah, I was ready for her this time. The day before, while I was on Yolana, I was practicing on how I would do Sheila! She called. I told her to come on down. I watched as usual. This time she had on a short brown top with some tan Calvin Klein's. I let her pass when she came in just so I could see her from the back. She looked good in her clothes. I was so used to seeing her in that *monkey-suit* at work. Instead of rushing things like the last time, I said,

"Have a seat."

She sat on the couch and I sat across from her in the recliner. I picked up the remote and we watched some BET. Keith Sweat was on the showcase trying to play that cool roll. After ten minutes, nothing happened. So she asked me to come and sit beside her. I played shy.

"I won't bite, Eric."

"I sure hope not." We both laughed. When the ice was broken, she came over to me.

"Now where am I supposed to fit in this little chair?"

"Anywhere you want to." I said in my sexiest voice. She looked impressed.

"M-m-m, I'll think of something." she said. Then she began undressing in front of me. Damn, that body! I was hard in a matter of seconds. Soon she was naked, and dang skippy I was too. I leaned back in the chair and watched her crawl on top and guide herself on me. She rode me like she was on a pogo stick. It hurt like hell though because she was so tight. It seemed like she got tighter with each stroke. Felt like my stuff was in a rat trap! After about a half an hour she came. I was too sore so I faked mine. The sacrifices you gotta make for a nut. As she walked to the bathroom, I watched that caramel coated body. I touched my stuff and the rest was history.

Yuk!

Chapter 3:

Organization

I HAD TO SET a schedule for myself. Mondays; Sheila, Tuesdays; Yolana, Wednesdays; Sheila, Thursdays and Fridays were Yolana's. I was doing it like mad! At work, Sheila and I had to play that stuff off hard. I did the same thing at school with Yolana. That was cool. I checked the mirror after sex each time. It looked like my mustache was growing. Maybe I wasn't so ugly like the girls in school used to say. They always said that about the unpopular guys. That was all right though, 'cause I was gettin' mine!

Later that week I was working the carryout register with Tammy. When she started giving me this look like I had done something. So, naturally, I asked her what she was up to.

"Nothing. You've got some nice lips though." What? I know that wasn't Ms. *you-too-young-for me,* giving me a compliment. I wasn't even goin' for that bull, so I mumbled a thank you.

"If only you were older boy....ungh!", she continued.

"Please Tammy, let's not go through this again o.k.? You know the deal with the kid so don't even come with that age crap."

"O.K.," she said, "then meet me in the walk-in freezer in three minutes." (Well then.)

I had to think of a way to get off line without Sheila seeing me. Got it! I purposely unplugged the sundae machine so I could go and fix it. There weren't any customers so I slid off line. When I got into the walk-in it was freezing! It had to have been twenty degrees Celsius in that mob! I could tell by the army of chill-bumps on my arms. Tammy was standing in the corner with her arms stretched open telling me to hurry up. I rushed over to her and we kissed passionately like we were on <u>The Young and the Restless</u>. As though releasing all that tension from last summer. It only lasted about ten seconds because we were scared and we knew it. Boy, if we got caught I couldn't even have imagined that. So we broke out of there quicklike. She grabbed a bowl of pre-shredded lettuce just to cover up. Tammy was cute, and I wanted to do her little ass, but she never showed much interest after that so.... oh well, her loss. I went back to Sheila and Yolana. It became a game. I would do Yolana in the shower after school, clean it up and do Sheila in the exact same place! Now this was more like it, I thought. My senior year was kickin'!

This went on for weeks. Straight on up until December. Man, it got cold. Quick like too. All the leaves had blown away, and we had a couple of inches of snow on the ground. Not much, but enough for Ma to make me shovel it. I reminisced on when I was little how my Dad and I would go out, throw snowballs, build snowmen, and best of all, make snowcream! Mama would tell us to go out, find the cleanest snow in the yard. Scrape a layer off the top and fill the bowl with the rest. Then she would put some milk, some sugar, and her *magic* potion in it. Her potion was actually vanilla extract. It took me one time to learn that, after my little slick behind drank some straight out the bottle trying to be Merlin! We three would just sit there eating snowcream and laughing while we thawed out. Yep, those were the days.

Anyhow, it was time for mid-term exams, and I had maintained a B+ Average. So I dismissed both of my 'freaks'. Well, actually I asked them for a little time off for educational purposes. I didn't play when it came to my grades. I knew I had to study, and I had to do it without interruptions. Ma helped me too. She'd pass by me in the house with little questions to quiz me.

"Baby, what's the Pythagorean Theory?"

"A squared plus B squared equals C squared, Mama."

"Good boy." she'd say, and I would sigh. Ma liked to drill me like that. Her questions weren't that hard because they came from *her* old tests.

"I before e except when?"

"After c."

"Second President of the U.S.?"

"John Adams." Damn I hated History. Half of what we were taught wasn't even true anyhow. Christopher Columbus didn't discover jack but somebody's back yard! How the hell do you walk in somebody's house and say "I know y'all live here, but we're just gonna be roommates." Abraham Lincoln, that's another one. Oh he was good. Yeah, I'm gonna free the slaves but they get no rights or property. Like there was a Slave-union! Stupid ass! And what about Thomas Edison? Sure you made the bulb flash, but did you sustain it so somebody could see at nightime? Hell naw! A brother did *that* too! Man, don't even get me started.

"Square root of 169, baby?"

"13, Ma."

"Year of the automobile?"

"Ma."

"What's a metaphor?"

"Ma!"

"How many sides to a decagon?"

"Ma!!!"

"Well I was just trying to help you baby, you don't have to yell."

"Thanks Ma. I love you."

When the exams came, I felt like I aced them. History was tough, but I expected that. I knew I had to pull my average up to at least an A- if I wanted to go somewhere like UNLV or anywhere else. I was tired of Charleston. Man I couldn't wait to go to college. I'd be gettin' booty every night!

After the last test, I had to give my brain a rest. I was off work that day too, so I brought Yolana over. Again. I wanted to try something different so I talked her into doing it on my dresser. I had seen these people doing that in a porno movie that Tyrone stole from his Uncle. It was a trip. Man, the people that do that stuff must not have bones. They'd be bending all over each other and everything. I wondered if they're having sex or playing twister! Yolana said she didn't like it when we finished. She said she was uncomfortable. She was just mad because she got dust on her butt cheeks. By the time she put her bra back on, I was behind her squeezing on her. She pulled her panties back down and we went at it. Halfway through, the phone rang. I was scared to answer my own phone for some reason.

"Hello, who is it?"

"Yo what's up Cooley!" It was only Tyrone. (Whew!)

"What'cha doin'?"

"Hngh? Uh...cooking."

"Cooking what Eric?" Like he was a detective or something.

"Food, chump, now what do you want, it's burning!"

I didn't want nobody in my biz'. Not even my main man Tyrone, with his big mouth. That mouth of his was how we became best friends anyhow. Back in the 6th grade, we had homeroom together. I noticed that he liked to doodle on paper while the teacher was talking just like I did! So we introduced ourselves and became buddies. Until that fateful day at the track. These older boys from another school came to ours and started picking on me. I gave one of 'em the bird and he hit me in my chest. Just when I was about to cry.............. I hear this loud scream from at least 50 yards off proclaiming,

"YEEEAH! Y'all gonna git it now! Y'all done messed with the wrong kid!"

At first, the bullies ignored him. Till he marched right up in their faces.

"Y'all must have a deathwish! Don't y'all know who he is?" Pointing directly at my face. "No? Well I'ma tell ya. That boy you just hit is Ole' man Joshua's son!"

Now, I didn't know who the hell he said I was, but it scared the crap out of those punks! I mean they turned and ran so fast, I didn't even see which way! When I asked who Ole' man Joshua was, Tyrone said he'd tell me later. Y'know he never told me. Anyhow, his mouth was too big to be in my "woman business". Friend or no friend. See that's how rumors get started. It was a false alarm though; he just wanted to go swimming Saturday

with the fellas. "Cool."

Chapter 4:

Growing Up

So it was me, Tyrone, his cousin Ron, and my other homeboy Phil. I'd known Phil since the 8th grade. He was chill. We went to the indoor pool in the Valley Springs complex where Ron lived. It was mostly populated by old people, so I guess you would have to be a real quiet person to live there. Oh well, so much for me. The lifeguard acting like he didn't want to give us the swim passes. I wanted to smack that chump. Some white people in the downtown areas made me sick with that. Like there's gotta be trouble when there's more than two of us. "Thank you, sir." Ron said intelligently. And that smart-ass lifeguard threw off and said, "Hey, no problem." Tyrone put his towel over my fist. I knew it wasn't worth it, but I wanted to clock him just once. Some people were so ignorant.

When we got in the pool, it was just as I thought. It was as if we were sharks, because everybody jumped out of that mob! That was cool with us, because now we had the whole damn pool. Ignorant folk. We were cuttin' the fool. I was waiting for the lifeguard to quiet us down, but when I looked over, he was gone too! Ron started doing cannonballs into the pool, but nobody noticed because he only weighed about a quarter! Ron was so skinny, he could use a rubberband for a belt! I was trying to float, but couldn't float for jack! I just didn't know how people could do that. Cool trick. Tyrone and Phil were still on the deck complaining about the cold water. I was just about to splash them good when Ron shouted, "That's her man!" We all looked up. That's when I saw her. I saw this fine lady walking inside the clubhouse! She was about 5'6" tall, on the heavy side, but all in the right places. When she got close enough for me to see her face I almost died. She was fine…as… hell! As she entered the pool gate, we spread like roaches. She seemed to be in her own world. She walked to the far side of the

35

pool, sat her towel down, laid back in the chair, put her headphones on, and closed her eyes. We were all staring at her. Her bathing suit was no joke either. It was black with a gold streak across it. I started doing my laps like I was in the Olympics. From slow to torpedo. I was getting cramps in my arms trying to impress this lady. The fellas tried their raps too. Everybody's voice dropped about two octaves. We were all sounding like Don Cornelius. That didn't work either. Not even a nudge.

"Go say something to her man?" Phil said.

"Bump that!" I retaliated. "I aint goin' out like 'Bob da boot!" I knew Ron was scared, so we looked to Tyrone. That mob didn't have any shame in his game! He got right up and walked his sloppy self right over to her. (Tyrone could even make swimming trunks look sloppy!) He stood directly in front of her. Purposely blocking her view. Oh boy.

That fool stood there and said, "Yo baby, what's your name?"

When she didn't respond, he annoyingly repeated himself. Much louder though. I held my breath. She stopped her walkman and opened her eyes as if a mosquito were pestering her. She calmly stood up, looked at Tyrone emotionlessly and said,

"It's definitely not baby."

And walked out like the room was empty.

Tyrone knew what was coming when he turned back around.

"Damn!"

"Yo, she dissed you!"

"I know that hurt your heart man!"

"Yo 'T', At least you can still beat yo meat!"

We screamed on him!

"Forget y'all man!" He replied. "Y'all chickens wasn't gonna say nothin'!"

He was right about that. The way she came in let me know she was out of my league. Well, at least I could dream about her. I did too. It was jacked up. I'd be thinking of her while I was on Sheila. And be thinking about Sheila while I was on Yolana! It wasn't that I needed to. It was just something to do. I didn't care either, 'cause I didn't talk in bed. Shoooot. Even if you're gonna be dumb, aint no point in being stupid!

I was back at work on the carry-out register. This customer pulled up to the menu screaming into the speaker. Man, I hated that mess! But I was supposed to play it cool, so I did.

"May I take your order please?"

"YEAH, GIMME A WHOPPER 'WIF' NO PICKLES AND A SMALL COKE!"

"I'm sorry sir, but we don't serve Coca-Cola, would you like a Pepsi instead?"

"Y'ALL DON'T HAVE COKE?"

(I just told you that dumb-ass!) "No sir we don't."

"AIIIGHT, GIMME THE PEPSI THEN!"

"Drive to the window please." I was ready to smack this mob. I got tired of dealing with stupid people like that. The car pulls up and this little "egg-headed" chump was driving. So I blew it off. When I reached down to get his money, guess who I saw? The lady from the pool! She was finer than I remembered. She was looking out of her window like she was totally disgusted. I was purposely stalling so I could get a better look at her.

"Your fries will be ready in a moment sir." He rolled his eyes. What was *she* doing with *that* guy? He couldn't have been rich, driving that old VW. So what was up? Damn, they looked like Vanessa Williams and 'Bert' from Sesame street! As I handed him his food, he saw that I wasn't looking at him. So he snatched the food and sped off. Punk.

Three days before Christmas break. Tisha had been calling me all week trying to hang out. I just didn't have the time though. Between school and the ladies, my schedule was booked. She caught me in the cafeteria though.

"Hey boy, I've been tryin' to reach you."

"Well you got me. What's up?"

"What's up is that you and I are going roller skating this Friday night right?"

"I don't know Tish'."

"What do you mean you don't know?"

"I don't know. I might have plans."

"Yeah, I know your plans Eric!"

(Oh hell... here we go again.)

"Yo, what's your beef girl?"

"You know damn well what it is boy! Ever since I introduced you to that ho', all you do is spend time screwing her!" (Needless to say, that pissed me off!)

"Don't give me that excuse Tisha! You're just mad because Aunt Jean won't let your black ass out of the house without me! And as far as who I'm doin' goes, I haven't seen a dude today that hasn't been between your legs!"

Normally we would laugh all of our disputes off, but that hurt her. As I knew it would. I'd never been that cruel to anyone I loved. She stared into my face with tear-filled eyes. Then she ran off.

"Tisha… Tisha!" I yelled after her. I noticed everybody watching me. Just then, I felt a pinch on my rear. It was Yolana.

"Hey baby, where you been lately?"

"Around."

"That's cool. So your place or mine today?"

"Neither." She wasn't catching on.

"Then where loverboy?" she persisted.

"Nowhere Yolana, damn!"

"What's the matter with you?" she asked, almost apologetically.

I had already blown up at Tisha. I didn't want to do it again.

"Yolana, can I call you later?"

"O.K. babe." she smiled.

Man, she didn't even know when she was being brushed off. That didn't matter though. What mattered was that I had just broken my baby cousin's heart. Over a piece of tail. I loved Tisha. She was my homegirl. We were tight ever since we were kids. We always had each other's back. I remembered way back in the 6th grade when this guy named Wesley's, sister tried to fight Tish' and got stomped. So then Wesley wanted to fight her himself and she told me. Boy, we beat him down! As big as he was, trying to fight girls. Of course I was *paranoid* until they finally shipped his big ass off to Reform School! He wasn't too bright. The point was, I'd stick my neck out for my cuz, and she'd do the same for me. We were tougher than leather together. I messed up. Bad.

After an eternity it seemed, I finally won back Tisha's heart. I was glad too, because my wallet couldn't take much more. Even after Christmas, I was getting her flowers, candy, taking her to every movie playing. I even bought her a stuffed elephant. 'Cause she damn sho' better had remembered that mess!

Things soon got back to normal as we stepped back into school. We got our mid-term grades. I got all B's and one A. (Yes!) Mom was very proud of her baby as usual. Tisha got straight D's. Damn, when Aunt Jean got through with her, her only method of communication was postal! It wasn't my fault. The girl just would not study. You can't just carry your books and expect your arms to just soak up the knowledge. You gotta open those mubs! Meanwhile, back at the carryout. I was getting tired. I'd been working that Saturday morning since 7 am., and it was almost 9pm . I called myself trying to get that OT. My throat was so dry, my mouth tasted like a Ritz cracker! So I poured myself a small sprite. I had just taken a swallow when 'BLEEP', another customer. Damn. Oh well.....

"Welcome to Burger King, may I take your order?"

The responding voice was smooth. The woman sounded like a DJ or an actress or something.

"Yes, may I have a large diet pepsi please?"

"Will that be all Mam?"

"Yes it will, thank you."

"Drive to the window please."

I was looking out the window as hard as I could. I was just dying to see the face behind that gorgeous voice. Oh smack, please let it be... please...yes! It was her! That lady from the pool again. And she was by herself. (Well then.) Man, I got nervous, but then I thought, she's only human, just talk to her. Cool. I knew she wouldn't rap to a Burger King worker anyway. So when she pulled up, I tried to treat her like any other customer. I smiled and said, "Hello."

"Hello." She smiled back!

"How are you?"

"I'm all right, just a little tired." She was wearing sweats, and she had a towel around her neck.

"If you don't mind me asking, where are you coming from?"

"It's all right. I'm coming from an aerobics class."

"That must be fun."

"Not for long it isn't. As soon as I get off this diet, I am out of there."

(Here I go.) "I'm on a diet too."

She chuckled in surprise.. "No seriously, I'm trying to lose weight."

"From where?"

"My feet. You can't see them, but trust me." She smiled. "See, I knew you had a pretty smile." I was having fun talking to her. She was a nice lady. "Well, I continued, I know you've got to be going and all, but it was nice talking to you." For a second it looked like she wanted to stay. She read my name tag and said,

"Well, Eric, I had a nice time talking with you also. You're certainly a pleasant young man." Not fully understanding, I thanked her. "You've got an attractive smile yourself. " I tried to cover my teeth with my lips. As she began to pull off, I blurted out.

"Wait, what's your name?!"

I froze. I was afraid she was going to do me like she did Tyrone. I didn't blink. She turned her head and said,

"It's Monica. Monica Simms."

"Well goodnight Mrs. Simms."

"It's Ms., and Monica will do."

That following week in school all I could think about was her. I couldn't get that pretty face out of my mind. I even drew pictures of her during my classes. I kept hearing that voice saying, "Monica will do." She was so pretty. I couldn't even begin to describe it. I kept hoping to see her at work. No show. After a few days, I was like, forget it, she aint never coming back. The week after, I was still thinking about her. I couldn't believe it. I couldn't shake her. Sheila got mad at me that week because I refused to work the fries. She had some nerve with that. She told me I was acting spoiled, but she knew not to push it. I mean, I figured it like this, eventhough she was my supervisor, I was doing the job her boyfriend wasn't, so I deserved a little *special* treatment. I knew you weren't supposed to mix business with pleasure, but I knew I could so I did.

Sheila got so mad with me that she stormed back to the office so she could do the inventory. *Whatever!* Just then I heard a voice say "Yes, him." Before I could turn, the cook tapped me on the shoulder and pointed to the front counter. When I looked, there was Monica. With her fine self. She waived at me like a little kid. I didn't oblige because I knew the entire crew was watching me. So I calmly walked over.

"Long time no see Ms. S-i- I mean Monica."

"Yes I know. How are you?" Damn she was so professional.

"O.K." I responded.

"I've been thinking about you Eric."

"Oh really?"

"Yes really. I couldn't shake that smile of yours."

All I could think to say was "Ditto". I peeped over the counter to see what she was wearing. She had on stonewashed jeans to match her denim shirt. She caught me staring.

"Do you like?" I was embarrassed. She saw it and smiled. "Well I have to go now Eric, but I'll be around."

"All right, I'll be looking for you." She winked as she walked to her car outside. Damn, I couldn't let her get away twice, not this time, I thought. At that I mumbled to the crew for someone to cover my register and darted outside after her. She was standing by her car looking for her keys.

"Monica?" She smiled as though she knew I'd come.

"Hi."

"Hey, listen I know I may be overstepping my bounds, but from what I know of you, I like you a lot." I didn't let her interrupt me. "Now I've got to go for what I feel is real. I'm not letting you get away again without at least trying...so would you please go to the movies with me sometime next week? Please?" I was scared as all. I realized how dumb I must've sounded, but it was too late.

"I thought you'd never ask Eric." My lips hit the ground.

"Say what?"

"I said, I'd love to go out with you."

I did my Fred Sanford heart-attack routine. She laughed.

"Do you have a phone?" I asked like a dummy.

"I think so."

"May I have your number please?" She just stared at me. "What? Did I say something wrong?"

"No Eric, with manners like yours, I don't think you could."

"Thanks, I try."

I wrote her name on a napkin and stuffed it back in my pocket.

"Is tonight all right to call you?"

"Tonight is fine."

I didn't know what to do then, so I reached out to shake her hand. She kissed me on my cheek! I felt dizzy. Then I ran back inside happy as all!

When I got back to the carryout, there were cars backed up to China! And guess who was standing right there? Sheila. (Oh hell.)

"Where have you been Eric?"

"Uh- I had to go to the bathroom. I asked someone to cover for me."

"Who'd you ask?"

"I said it to the whole crew."

"The bathroom huh?"

"Yes Sheila, the bathroom." I wasn't budging. Neither was she. She stared me in the eyes, walked right up to me, pulled me down and whispered in my ear.

"Then what the hell is that on your face!"

Busted…cold busted. Naw, snagged like a motha! Any way you put it, that was messed up. Sheila was madder at me than she was at Mike! She didn't say two words to me for a week. I hated it too, because that was half of my *booty surplus*!

So I called Monica.

"Hello, who's calling?" she said with that sexy voice.

"Hi Monica, it's me Eric." I said in my studliest voice. I'm glad she giggled because I couldn't hold the voice that long. We talked for a good hour and a half. I asked if she had a boyfriend.

"No I don't." (Yes!)

"That's great Monica, I don't have a boyfriend either!"

We talked about past experiences. We agreed on the fact that alot of times partners tend to put unneeded pressures on you.

"I don't appreciate it when a man smothers me."

"Word, and I don't like it when a woman constantly wants to keep watch on you like you're some kind of stray dog." I liked talking to her. We set a date for the movies on Saturday. Winter was almost gone, so it was a great opportunity to spring out my new sports jacket.

"Well, goodnight Monica."

"Goodnight sugar."

Man, how I had the hots for that woman!

When I hung the phone up, I was still thinking about Sheila. Man, that was rough. Then I thought, wait a minute! She's got a man and she's gonna cop an attitude with me over something she doesn't even understand? *Hells naw.* I couldn't be going for that. If we were gonna play games, then we're gonna play mine. Man, I wasn't no whore. And that's exactly what I told her the next day.

"And furthermore....., I'm not just some piece of meat you can have anytime you want a snack! If you wanted me that bad, you'd have broken up with Mike by now. Right?" She didn't speak. "Look Sheila, maybe we should just stop this now. I don't want to get you into any trouble, and I definitely don't want Mike to try to kill me!"

"You're so crazy Eric." she laughed. "You're right and I'm sorry. Can we talk about this at your place after work?" (Now that was more like it!)

"How about next week?" I asked.

"Why next week?"

"Sheila."

"Nevermind. Next week it is."

Saturday night Monica and I met at the Cineplex II Theater. It wasn't even crowded. Normally, brothas bring their entire families on Saturdays. "Bloodsport" was playing in Theater I. "Ghost" was in the other. I had seen "Ghost" so many times, I thought I was in that mob! I really wanted to see the new one anyway. I loved some karate. When we got to the token booth, I figured she'd want me to decide for the both of us, but I wasn't sure. Oh well, "Two for "Ghost" please." She made no expression. When I opened the door for her she smiled and shook her head in disbelief.

"Would you like any snacks Monica?"

"I'll split a box of raisinets with you."

"Alright." I said with a smile.

"Oh, and Eric? I'd also like....."

"A large diet pepsi." we said at the same time.

It was pitch dark in the theater. I asked her to hold on to my shirt until we found a seat. It was small and secluded inside. I liked that. I didn't want her to let go when we sat down. I also didn't want to screw it up, so I chilled. Halfway through the movie, I started to get cold. I should've brought in my jacket, but oh no, not my cool ass.

"Are you cold Monica?"

"Not really." I touched her hand, it was freezing!

"Not cold huh?"

"Well maybe just a little." I instinctively pulled her into my arms.

"How's that?"

"Much better."

Damn, she felt good in my arms. I wished they were longer. That way I could've wrapped them around her whole body.

"You're cute lady, did you know that?"

"Well thank you sir." she said, with a royal accent. With that, I pecked her on the cheek. In turn she reached around my neck and kissed me like I'd *never* been kissed. Her lips were so soft. Her tongue was like honey. When we pulled away, we just stared at each other. Then we did it again.

"Let's go somewhere Eric."

"Where?"

"How about your place?" I shook my head no because I knew Ma was home.

"Then let's go to mine."

We left right then and there. Man…. damn a ghost! Before we got to our cars, we were at it again. First at her car, then at mine. Finally, she got in her car and said, "Follow me." I was driving like a madman! The usual. I wouldn't let any other car get between us. Because if I lost her, that would've been somebody's neck that night. I was focused on her licensee plate. "AZT-080". She turned into this nice apartment complex. When we parked, I had to stay in my car for a moment. The remix of Bobby Brown's "Roni" was on. That song was the jazz. I saw her waiting for me so I hopped out. I couldn't believe this was happening! When I walked inside, I almost flipped out. The place was fresh! The kitchen matched the livingroom. The glass table matched the coffee tables. The carpet was all nice and velvet looking. Damn, I bet the roaches wore Sunday shoes in that mob!

"Nice place." I complimented.

"Thank you."

"How many bedrooms?"

"Just one."

"Then where do your parents sleep?" (That slipped.)

"Oh I don't….well…. I live alone."

How in the hell could she afford this place? Damned if I was asking. I looked at her pictures on the walls. She looked *fly* in every one of them. She went to get me a drink. Diet pepsi of course. She should've bought stock in that company as much as she drank it. She even had a fireplace with brass antiques and stuff around it. When I checked the shelf above, I couldn't believe my eyes. This woman had all kinds of degrees and certificates from UNC-Chapel Hill, University of South Carolina, and North Carolina Central University. One was for Accounting, and from the looks of that place, she made much money! When she brought my drink, I asked her what she did for a living.

"I'm an accountant."

I played like I was interested as she explained exactly how this amount of money had to be managed so you could whatever. She was way over my head, and it bothered me.

"What's wrong Eric?"

"What's wrong?" I didn't hesitate. "What's wrong is that you're like, "I'm an accountant". What do I say? Hi, I'm a burger flipper."

She tried not to laugh because she saw I was serious. When she composed herself, she took me by the hand and sat me on the couch.

"Now I want you to listen to me. Eric, you are...you're special. You're unique. You use common sense. You make me feel like a lady. Like I have a brain, a choice, and not just an exterior. I thought there were no more like you on the planet. I had given up. But then here you come with that smile." (I smiled) "And you blew my mind. Therefore, I couldn't care if you sold toilet tissue for a living. You make me happy, and I'd like to make you happy." She was serious too. She led me to her bedroom door. I couldn't have imagined what was on the other side. She had a queen sized waterbed with a mahogany oak frame and headboard. It even had lights on it. And on top of all that, she had black satin sheets. (Aw yeah!) She had the nice bedroom. The dressers and chairs were mahogany like the bed frame. It was right out of one of those catalogs. Then she walked over to her Sony component system and put in one of those new 'CD' disks. I waited for the results. It was Barry White. (Awww.....sookie sookie now!)

She smiled and said, " The bathroom is straight across the hall."

For what? I thought. Then my conscience spoke to me. (Who gives a damn? Just get your ass in there!) So I went. She had a small tray on the right side of the sink with three different colored condom packets in it. Damn she was smooth. I washed my *jimmy* and put on the red Trojan. Just because red was my favorite color. Actually they were called Lady Trojans. Why, I had no clue. I came out of the bathroom with nothing but my draws on. My heart was jumping. (Get a grip boy!) I knocked on her door.

"Come in."

She had dimmed the lights, lit incense, and changed into a lace body suit. (I-be-damned!!) She just didn't quit! She was lying on her bed like a centerfold model. She blew a kiss to me. Man………. My thing was so hard, you could've built a birdhouse on it! I felt hypnotized. I didn't know what to do or how to start. I just know I didn't want to screw up. That's all I could think of. So I laid down beside her and tried to kiss her entire body. And I mean every inch. I had never done that before. It was like taboo or something. I couldn't have her thinking she was with no teenager. I wanted her. I wanted her bad. Wanted to do my best. I brushed her hair with my hand. Licked her lucious lips. Went down and unbuttoned the midsection of her suit. Took my time coming back up. Then, ecstasy! I felt like King Triton on that waterbed. She was a big lady, but it wasn't the size of the ship, it was the motion of the ocean! We did it until we fell asleep.

6:15a.m. Sunday morning. My alarm clock went off as usual. I promised Ma I'd go to church with her. I could hear the DJ talking about sunny weather, with his fake *New York* accent. I reached to the right to turn it off, but it wasn't there. When I opened my eyes, I couldn't believe them. Monica was lying on my chest! Oh smack! What the----! Oh man, this was too deep for me. I mean, I'd had sex before, but I'd never slept with anyone! I thought that only happened on television. It kinda felt cool so I put my arm around her. I wanted to see her face. I moved her hair aside. She was fine as the first time. I didn't know women could look good in the morning. Well, at least not that good. I sat there motionless for ten minutes, thinking of some excuse to tell Ma. I'll tell her I went to a party and got too tired to drive back. Then why didn't I call? Damn, I'm screwed. Oh well, might as well make the best of it. I tried to reach the clock before it woke Monica, but it was too late. I watched her as she opened her eyes. I greeted her with a smile. She smiled back.

"Good morning."

"Good morning, love." She kissed me on my chest. "Last night was nice."

Nice? I almost broke the small of my back trying to serve her and she says nice? Well, maybe that's what she was supposed to say. So I responded with, "Yes, it was."

She kissed me again, this time on the lips and eased off of the bed. She took one of the sheets and wrapped it around her. She made it look like an evening gown almost. It really brought out her breasts too. I really didn't notice how nice they were until then. They were huge. They made Yolana's look like sunflower seeds! I couldn't control my erection. She saw the bulge under the spread. Then she touched him and he sprang to life.

"Would you like a little before breakfast?"

"I'd love some."

She pulled the covers off and climbed on. Not like Sheila did though. Monica was patient with it. It was so good I could've cried. When she got out of the shower, she started getting ready for work. This situation was blowing my mind! I just sat on her bed with my mouth wide open. Her closet was full of nice clothes. She was definitely paid in full.

"Can I do anything to help, Monica?"

"Yes, could you make me a quick cup of coffee, hun?" Oh snap, so now I'm hun!

I always made Ma coffee with the little saucepan on the stove, but Monica had a new "Instant Coffee Maker." I didn't want to sound stupid asking for instructions. So by the time she came out, I had boiled it on the stove like Ma always did, and put the filter in the sink like I had used it. Damn, I was a genius! I handed her the coffee with loving eyes. She didn't like it, but she tried to play it off. She held the cup for ten minutes, but took one sip. She had on this nice olive green business suit. The skirt came just short of her knees. She set the coffee on the counter and led me to her door. I was still in my socks, and I was looking for my shoes. She pulled me to her and laid another one of her *knockout* kisses on me. Then she said, "Just lock the door from the inside before you leave." (Say what?) Then she left. Now I'm standing in this woman's apartment like, what just happened? I mean, what if I was a thief or something? I scoped her pad up and down. In search of what, I had no idea. She had such nice things. I guess it meant something to have your own place. I looked through her CD's. She had a lot of the same jams I had. Heavy D and the Boyz, Bobby Brown, Guy, Chaka Khan, all of them. I didn't mess with anything else, because she had trusted me. Besides, I knew I had to get home. I straightened up before I left. Double-checked her door and stepped out like Superman.

I hit the beltline flying! By the time I came off the ramp good, I saw a police car in my rearview. I knew he was going to try me. So I floored it for the next exit. He turned on his siren and took the bait. I weaved through traffic, got off and pulled around the underpass. I watched his *doughnut -poppin' ass* speed right on by. Some cops *iz* so.... stupid!

When I got home, Ma was still there. She was waiting for me. And that's when it really hit the fan.

"Where in the hell were you last night, boy?!"

Big trouble. In my lifetime I'd only heard Ma curse twice. The time Dad's stupid ass girlfriend called the house, and when Dad's stupid ass tried to slap her. I'd never forget that. He boldly admitted that he was cheating and told Ma that she had better get used to it. Ma told him to get out and that fool took a swing at her. Ma went straight to the kitchen and brought out a big ol' economy sized jar of jelly and **clocked** him with it. He ran out holding his head. Then she held me to her and cried.

"Did you hear what I said boy?!"

"Yes Mam."

"Well?" Tapping her foot.

"I went to a party and got too tired to drive home."

"Why didn't you call then?" (Damn!)

"I-I-forgot."

"You forgot? You didn't forget to bug me about that car until you got it did you...? **I said did you?!?**"

"No Mam." I said, hanging my head.

"I know you didn't. And the next time you leave this house and worry me sick all night, your black ass will be on the freeway on skates! Now do I make myself clear?"

"Yes Mam."

"I can't hear you!"

"Yes Mam!"

"Boy, don't you raise your voice at me. You may be tall, but I'll sling your butt all over this house!" I wanted to mumble something, but Mama didn't raise no fool! I knew I was up the creek without a boat. "Now get out of those raggedy clothes and get ready for church."

"Aw man!"

"What did you say?"

"Nothing Mother."

"Don't try me boy."

Right before we left for church, Ma stopped me at the door.

"Oh so now you hate Mama right? She does her best for you, but you hate her guts, huh?"

"Ma."

"That's alright, you work hard all day, come home and slave over a hot stove..."

"Ma!"

"I can still put you up for adoption you know."

"Ma!!"

"What?"

"I love you O.K.?"

"That's my baby." I couldn't resist her open arms. I loved her. No matter how mad she made me or I made her. I knew that she would always love me. I didn't understand why she was so mad. She had fear in her eyes. I was scared for *her*. I never wanted to make my Mama cry. She was my best friend in the whole world for goodness sake. Oh boy, how am I gonna get out of this one. If being grown can cause that much stress over other folk then I'm staying a kid. Dang all that worrying about other folk.

Chapter 5:

The Church

"....AND THAT'S THE PROBLEM with God's children nowadays..., they're scared!" When we got in, Rev. Howard was going off! "That's right, I said it, just down right chicken! Scared to say no to folks. Scared to stand up for themselves. Scared to speak to folks. And then gonna sit up in here every Sunday talkin' about, Amen Preacher!" (*Well!*) I heard from the left and the right. "You see, there is and has always been a huge misconception about Christians." (*Watch out now!*) Yes, Jesus has taught us to turn the other cheek, but he don't say put your face out to be slapped!" (*Well!*) "Brother's and sisters, following the Word of God doesn't mean being gullible. Stop trying to make everybody happy. Stop trying to be everybody's friend. Jesus is the best friend you can ever have!" (*Amen!*) "I don't think y'all hear me." (*Glory! Glory!*) Even Ma went off! "Let me ask y'all something." He lowered his voice and wiped his brow. "When Jesus walked into the Temple and saw the men gambling and trading and selling and whatnot, do you think he said, could you please leave?" (*No!*) The congregation responded. "No! He said, GET OUT! And family I want you to know today that if Satan is in your life, you rebuke him in the name of Jesus, and tell him to GET OUT! If Satan is controlling your marriage!" (*GET OUT!*) Everybody yelled. "If he's in the minds of your children!" (*GET OUT!*) "If he's in your household." (*GET OUT!*) "Lawd ha' mercy! The Word of God is quick and powerful, and sharper than any two-edged sword." (*Yes sir!*) Then he laughed to himself. "And whomever don't like it in here.......... GET OUT!"

Man, Rev. Howard should've run for President or something. He was pretty cool, for a Preacher.

The next day in school I found out that they'd be holding the SATs soon. Oh brother, the Aptitude tests. That's when they find out who really knows their stuff and who hangs out with Tisha. I didn't know what to study or anything. I panicked. So I called Yolana afterschool.

"Hello?"

"What's up Yo'?"

"Hey Eric, long time no call."

"Aw girl, I call you all the time."

"No you don't Eric so don't even...."

"Anyway, what are you doing?"

" Nothin' but baby-sitting my little sister."

"That girl is eleven years old!"

"So?"

"So can I come over?"

"If you want to."

"Cool, I'm on my way."

"Hurry."

When I got there, there were two other little girls over.

"Who are these two?" I asked Yolana.

"Oh these are my sister's friends, LaToya and LaSonya."

They looked more like simple and simon. I said hi to the girls and they started giggling. I hated it when girls did that. I hated it when grown women did that. Females, no matter what age will always bond against you. Brothers are too damn macho to tell each other their problems. Oh well. I moved Yolana to the kitchen and asked her if I could have some. She said she didn't think so because of the girls. Her mother told her not to let her sister outside. The other two didn't want to go home. After minutes of thought, I came up with the master plan. Hide 'N' Seek in the house. No kid could resist that. So while they seek, we can hide in the basement and get busy! Yolana laughed at my brilliance.

"So, are you down or what?"

"O.K. Eric, but if we get caught, I know she'll tell it."

"We aint gonna get caught girl."

I asked the kids if they wanted to play and they jumped for joy. The first game, I was *it*. So I counted to fifty. I knew exactly who I wanted to catch. LaToya. She wore glasses, but couldn't see a thing past five feet. She reminded me of Velma from <u>Scooby Doo.</u> It took me all of ten seconds to catch her. She hid behind a glass coffee table.

Ray Charles could've found her. I told her to count to 100. When she started, her sister ran to the same spot. Kids. They think that if you don't say anything then you don't know anything. Yolana's sister, Ebony, ran upstairs. We raced to the basement and started taking our clothes off. I could hear counting away upstairs. By the time she reached twenty, we were going at it! I had to put my T-shirt in her mouth so we wouldn't get caught.

"33...34!" I was sweating like a dog. I had her legs over my shoulders and I was ramming her like she stole something. She felt good. When I heard LaToya say 82, I was getting ready to explode. Man that was some sticky business. "95...96!" We got our clothes back on and tried to wipe off the sweat. I was too tired to run so I let LaToya catch me.

When I got back home, it was about 4:30p.m. The phone was ringing. I rushed to get it because I hated missing calls.

"Hello?"

"Hello baby."

"Hey Ma!"

"What are you so excited about boy?"

"Nothing, it's just good to hear from you."

"Ungh, anyway. Lay out the chicken in the freezer so it'll be thawed when I get home."

"Yes Mam."

"Oh, and Eric, don't forget......"

"Mam?"

"Mama loves you."

Ah-h-h now that was sweet. I went and put the chicken in the sink. It dropped like cement. It was almost five and there was nothing to do. I had just done Yolana, Sheila was in school, and Monica was at work. So I called Tyrone to see what he was up to. He said he was preparing for his SATs in advance. I was shocked. After three years of highschool he was finally coming around. So I decided to just go for a drive. Just cruise the town. I put in Michael Jackson's "BAD" tape and "Smooth Criminal" came on. (Aw heck!) I started screaming my "woo's" and "hee-hee's" and of course I grabbed my *jammy*. People thought I was nuts on the road. I pulled into a Wendy's to get a frosty cup. We had the whopper, but we couldn't touch their frosties. So I was a traitor. I decided to go through the drive-thru so I could get it and go. Damn. Their line was longer than ours was! I didn't sweat it though because I knew the horror of the carry-out. When I finally got to the window, the register worker looked totally disgusted. Just like I did after a few hours on that mob. Her name was Sinobia. I smiled at her and said, "It's not easy is it?" She shook her head no.

"Don't worry, you'll make it."

"Thanks."

"My name is Eric."

"Hi, I'm Sinobia." I shook her hand.

"Nice to meet you."

"You too."

After a few seconds of the "Eric charm," I got her phone number. She was cute, but looks are deceiving. Come to find out, homegirl was seventeen, lived with her boyfriend, who coincidentally had been in jail twice, and had two children! I had to hang up on her before she asked me to the prom! I was out like a breeze through the trees.

Chapter 6:

Buckling Down

ALL WEEK IN SCHOOL it was test here, quiz there. I guess it was to prepare us for the SAT. I knew it wouldn't be easy so I had to buckle down. Sheila called me every day that week claiming that she wanted to talk. Yeah, right. I mean, normally I would've let her come over, but not that week. I called Monica and explained to her, that I would be busy that week. She was very understanding. I didn't have to worry about Yolana. She was on her period. Yeah, guys keep up with that also. We may not remember birthdays and anniversaries, but we remember that. I knew I had to get a good grade. And in order to do that, I had to work hard.

7:45 a.m. Saturday morning. SAT day. I had a headache from studying last night. I had two and a half hours to wash up, eat breakfast, and get out with time to spare. I always made time to spare because I hated rushing. Y'see when you rush, you tend to forget the important things. I made it to the school at 10:30a.m. It was packed. It looked like the fairgrounds. I saw a lot of my classmates, and a lot of unfamiliar faces. Then I remembered, this was a county-wide testing site. The schedule I got in the mail said to go to room 128A. I knew that room like the back of my hand. That was my Algebra II room. Except there was a little old man sitting there instead of Mrs. Kidd. He read the student list and everyone was present. They better had been for $30 a seat, shoot. He asked if we needed #2 pencils. A few students raised their hands. We filled out our bubble sheets. I loved that part. Then we all went to the bathroom. When we got back and the clock struck 11:00a.m., the last thing I heard was.... "You may begin."

When the test was over, I was so glad. It wasn't as hard as I thought it would be though. Everybody sighed. It was time to go and I was ready to *git*. But when I tried to get up, I couldn't. My knees had gotten stiff on me. So instead of jumping up and bustin' my butt, I stayed there playing it off like I was in deep thought. It had gotten hot outside. So when I got to my car, I was gonna jump in and crank up the A/C. Man, when I opened my door it was like Martha and the Vandellas, a "Heat Wave." It was so hot in my car; it was like I had the Devil in the backseat! There was no way I was gettin' in there, so I rolled down my windows and stood there. Chillin'. Then and old familiar face walked by. "Vanessa? Vanessa Douglas?" She turned and stared at me for a second and then recognized me.

"Eric Monroe, is that you?"

"It's me." I walked over and gave her a hug. "Hey girl, I remember you from the 9th grade." My 9th grade year I went to Strathmore High school with Vanessa, because we hadn't moved yet. Vanessa was busted then, but man, three years can work miracles on you! But you don't tell women stuff like that. So I said, "You still look good Vanessa." It went straight to her head just like I knew it would.

"Thanks, I haven't changed much. You look a lot different Eric."

"Is that a compliment?"

"Of course it is boy."

"Thanks, are you driving? Do you need a lift?"

"Actually, I'm waiting for my mother."

"I could take you." I insisted.

"She should be on the way by now."

"O.K., well can I call you sometime?"

"Sure you can." she smiled. "I'd give you my number if you'd let me go." (Oh, smack I was still hugging her!) "What time is it?" she asked.

"2:15."

"Dag!"

"What?"

"I told my mother 3:00."

"Good. That gives us a little time."

"A little time for what?"

"Y'see how you think Vanessa, I just wanna talk."

"We're talking now."

" Same ol' smart mouth." We laughed together.

"I'm just playing with you Eric."

We sat in my car reminiscing the old days. She was diggin' my ride. I drove her around the corner to our football field. She asked me if she could drive. Yeah right!! She had about as much of a chance driving my car as a Ku Klux Klan member streaking in Harlem! So anyway, after shootin' the breeze, I tried her.

"Y'know Vanessa, I've always liked you."

"You have?"

"Yeah, you just looked so good, I thought you would never give me a chance."

"Really?"

"Really......... and I don't know when I'll see you again ...so can I have a kiss?" She didn't blink.

"O.K. Eric, but just on the cheek."

"All right."

Within minutes her tongue was in mouth. My hands had made their way under her shirt. She had her hand right on my crotch! I slid my hand down to maybe unzip her pants. She had already unzipped them! Her hair was so soft and curly. I liked playing in it. I knew we would run out of time so I didn't even try to go further. She wanted to though. Bad. I couldn't be rushin' my groove in my car. I didn't have any rubbers either. I would have wound up nuttin' on my interior screwin' up the dashboard. I didn't need the stress. However, my fingers were getting their money's worth. She was wet. The stickier my fingers got, the more I wanted to go ahead and do her. Oh well. When her mother pulled up, I waved to her. She didn't recognize me. She waved back anyway. Vanessa told her who I was, and she called me a nice boy.

Sunday morning, I had to open the store with Sheila. I got there at 6:40p.m.Twenty minutes early. The place was deserted. I started dozing off after a few, so I popped in my N.E. Heartbreak tape. By the time Sheila drove up, I was jammin'! I got out of my car and danced over to hers.

"Come on girl, shake yo' thang!"

"You so silly Eric."

I didn't even notice the passing cars watching me cut the fool in the parking lot. Inside the store was spotless...which was highly irregular for the night-shift. Still there was much to do. Sheila handed me the keys to the freezer and I grabbed her arm.

"Can I have my morning kiss now?" She kissed me. "Is that all I'm gonna get?"

"What are you talking about?"

"C'mon Sheila, we're all alone."

"Yeah, and we've got work to do."

I moved in for the kiss. She didn't push me away. In fact, she gave me that tongue. I liked that. My watch said 7: 20a.m. which gave us twenty minutes before the dayshift came in. I reached under her shirt to unbutton her bra. All her bras opened from the front. It took me awhile to get used to that. She even let me unzip her pants! The next thing I knew, I had her on the counter and I was between her legs. She was still tight. Doing it in Burger King. Damn. I didn't even care. As nice as her body was, I could've done her on the roof. When I told her I was coming, she was like... "No, Eric.... not now baby!" Not now? I couldn't help it with that padlock booty. I pulled out and nutted on a cheeseburger wrapper. We cracked up! We eventually got it together and did some work. Sheila didn't even want me to look at her funny. She was so nervous. I played with her anyway. When she'd walk by, I'd hold up a cheeseburger wrapper. She didn't laugh, but I thought that was hilarious!

Chapter 7:

"The Gyrlz"

THE LUNCH HOUR WAS rough! People were coming out of nowhere. We had a 99-cent special on our Burger Buddies. They were buying those things up. One guy ordered ten of'em! I'm glad I wasn't on the grill. Even so, the carry-out was getting on my last nerve. People yelling in my speaker, snatching their food, and running out of patience. Boy they just didn't know what I went through. Maurice had been on my back all day. Sometimes I wished I was the manager and he was the employee. I'd have that mub doin' push-ups in front of the customers! He called me over to cover the front register while he conducted an interview in the dining area. I watched him to see who he was going to sit with. There was this nice looking lady out there, but he passed her. (Damn!) Suddenly, he turned and looked directly at me and snagged me. He always seemed to catch me when I wasn't working. But when I was *slaving*, his dumb ass was nowhere to be found. I had to play it off though.

"Maurice, I need your keys."

He looked at me like, yeah right. He brought me the keys anyway. I purposely over-rang an order and kept watching him. He sat down with these two little girls. And I mean little. They were almost smurfs! Who were they? I knew he wasn't interviewing *those* little girls. By the time I took care of the last customer, I saw him shaking their hands. Then they left. I was curious.

"Yo, Maurice, who were they?"

"Yo, Eric, don't worry about it."

Chump. Naw, 'Reese was all right. I was just like the son he never had or something. He just got on my nerves. I didn't need that crap. I had a daddy. I barely ever saw him, but he was still my dad. Tyrone's cousin, Ron, never even saw his dad. That's screwed up. He probably found out his mom was pregnant and left. Man, I would've never done anything like that. If the girl got pregnant I wouldn't leave. I'd help her get the money for the abortion.

When I got back to work Monday, I saw the two little girls in there with oversized uniforms on. They looked like they didn't know where they were. I went on to the back to clock in. Cliff, the cook, was like... "Yo man, did you see them fly girls up front?"

"Man, those girls are young."

"E, I don't even care, them butts is fat!"

"You sick Cliff."

When I got to my register, Dave, our lunch manager, introduced us. Cyndi and Kim. Cyndi was light complexioned and Kim was a dark brown complexion. That seemed to be the only way to tell them apart. Dave said, "Eric, I'm going to show Cyndi here the dining room. I want you to teach Kim the carry-out register." They looked at each other in fear for a moment. As though being torn apart forever. As Dave took Cyndi, I made a sad baby face and waved 'bye-bye' to her. She waved back. As soon as I looked back to Kim she said, "You like Cyndi?"

"Excuse me?"

"Do you like my friend Cyndi?"

"Sure--I--guess, but probably not how you're thinking."

"Well, do you think she's pretty?"

"I think you're both pretty."

"Then which one of us do you like?"

I could tell she was young. 15 max, but I wasn't even thinking that way. And I didn't want to start off on the wrong foot.

"Look Kim, you're pretty. So is Cyndi. So are five billion other women on the planet, but that doesn't mean I want anything from you. O.K.? I just don't think like that."

"Then what do you think?"

I pinched her cheeks. "I think you're cute." She smiled, but she got the point. Besides, I was gonna be 18 in three weeks!

"Now this is the register. Can you say, re--gi--ster? The register is our friend." She laughed. She had a cute smile.

"How tall are you?" she asked.

"I'm 6'1. How tall are you?"

"I don't know." She shrugged. I put her shoulder to my stomach and said,

"You're about 6'."

"Yeah right."

She couldn't have been any taller than five feet. So I taught her the register. She learned quickly. I even let her take an order or two. Of course I had to adjust the microphone so she could reach it. She was really cool. It was like having a kid sister. I liked that.

That night, I called Monica.

"Hello?"

"Hello Monica, this is Eric."

"Hi sugar." (Damn, that voice!)

"Would you mind a little company?"

"Not at all, do you remember the way?"

"How could I forget?"

I told Mama I was going to a friend's house and that I would call when I got there and before I left. She o.k.'d it and I was gone. I got there in 17 minutes. It's normally a 30 minute drive. I ran up her steps and rang the doorbell. She opened the door looking drop-dead gorgeous! She had on this white full-length dress with white heels.

"Wow, you look great!" I said without thinking.

"Thank you sir."

"Are you going out somewhere?"

"No. I just wanted to know what you thought of this dress."

Once I sat down, I asked to see her runway walk. She pretended like a high fashion model with her nose in the air. She sure could've been.

"Man, I'd sure like to be that dress."

"Oh you would?" She came over to me and kissed me. Then she tried to back away, but my arms were already around her.

"Where are you going?"

"Well, I was going to slip out of this dress."

"Well, let me help you." I peeled her shoulder straps as though peeling a banana. I kept on peeling until her voluptuous breasts were in sight. They were beautiful. Their size, their shape, their feel. Her skin was so smooth. Man, it's just something about a woman's body! Maybe I should've taken up dermatology. I cupped those babies and went to *suckville*. When her nipples got hard, that aroused me even more. I was even harder than the last time. I stood up to go and get a condom. Right before I took a step... it happened. Monica knelt in front of me, unzipped my pants, and put it in her mouth! I couldn't believe this was happening. I had never experienced anything like oral sex before. I mean, I talked noise with the rest of the fellas…but dang! I felt so dizzy, I had to hold on to the arm of her couch. After a few moments, I felt myself about to explode! I panicked. I yanked it out of her mouth and came in my hand. (Yuk!) It was a lot too.

"I-- I'm sorry Monica."

"What for?"

"For not telling you I was about to come."

"I knew you were going to."

"Yeah, but if I didn't pull, it would've been in...."

"I know Eric."

(Oh so it's like that?) I went to the bathroom and turned my hand upside down. It came off like cold syrup. I was disappointed when I came out. And she actually asked me what was wrong.

"I still wanted to do the nasty with you, but my man's so limp now, you could use him for fishbait."

"Not a problem." she said, with extreme confidence.

"Oh yeah, that's easy for you to say."

She smiled at me and walked to the kitchen. I heard her freezer door open and shut. I had to see what she was doing. She had pulled out two ice cubes, and she was holding them in her hands. Then she turned the hot water faucet and ran the water over her hands until the ice dissolved. (What the hell?)

Then she walked over to me and cupped my crotch. I could feel the cold all the way through. I could also feel my nature rising. By the time she stopped kissing and massaging me, I was bulging. Damn, where did she get an idea like that from? I had heard of some, but that one took the cake! She went to her bedroom to set the scene, so I snuck and called Ma. Ma was like, "Don't forget where you live." Ma was a trip. So then, I went on my *rubber run*. I tapped on her door.

"May I come in now?"

"You certainly may."

This woman had changed into a red teddy! It even had the garter things! My mouth hit the floor. She raised her arms in the air.

"Well aren't you going to frisk me?" That was my cue. That was also the last thing I remembered that night.

7:00 a.m. The alarm clock went off. I reached high and over so I wouldn't hit Monica, but she wasn't there. I opened my eyes. I was in my own room. How did I get there? No time to think about that, I was running late for school. I dashed out the door with a nappy head. I just made it in time, but I couldn't find a parking space to save my life. As a result, I got to first period late. I didn't even feel like making up an excuse, so I just took my seat. Detention Hall. This girl named Freda was staring at me like I passed gas or something.

"Did you lose something Freda?"

"Nope." she said, smirking at me.

"Then, turn your nosey butt back around." I whispered. She rolled her eyes.

"That'll be enough Eric!" Mrs. Turner threatened.

"Yes mam."

"Now class, I'm sure you are all eagerly anticipating your SAT results." The whole class sighed. "Well I'm sure you all did just fine."

Some students complained, but I didn't care. I felt good about the test. And if I screwed up, then I'd just take it over.

I passed Yolana in the hallway and she pinched my butt.

"After school?"

"Naw. I got D-Hall."

She laughed.

"Shut up girl." I laughed too.

"I'll wait for you." Cool.

It was only thirty minutes. She waited too. With her cute self. I kissed her as soon as we got in the car. When we got to the house, I told her I wanted something different. She had never gotten on top, so I asked her to ride me.

"Ride you?"

"Yeah girl, jump on up here."

Boy, would I ever regret those words. There I was, lying butt-naked and erect, waiting for her to climb on top. This girl literally jumped on my stuff! And she thought it was funny when I screamed! That stuff pissed me off big time!

"Yo girl, what the heck do you think this is, "<u>Blazing Saddles</u>"?!"

"Sorry." she giggled.

"Sorry?! You almost break my willy and you say sorry?" She hung her head. "Just get off me Yolana. Damn!"

"I said I was sorry. I didn't know. I…"

"Alright!" I tried not to express my anger, because I still wanted some sex. "Just lay down Yolana."

"O.K."

I did her anyway with what little meat I had left. Then I took her home without two words. Then I came back and got ready for work. I couldn't find my Bobby Brown tape, so I popped in GUY. "Piece of My Love" came on. I was singing that mob too. "*Baby, you can't have all of me / 'cause I'm not totally free/ I can't tell you everything that's going on.*" When I got to work, I saw Cyndi and Kim.

"Hey Eric." Kim said.

"Hiya doll!" I replied. Cyndi just stared.

"Afternoon Cynthia." I said with a British accent. She tried to hold it, but failed. Then she tried to play it off by coughing, and eventually waved. I saw Sheila in the office, but I didn't look her way. As soon as I punched in, she was in my face.

"Hello Mister."

She wanted to get together after work. I was with it, but I was still sore from Yolana playing 'The Lone Ranger' on my jammy. I should've kicked her out.

"Maybe another time Sheila, O.K.?"

"You said that last time Eric, and the time before that!"

"Now don't get upset Sheila…….."

"I'm not upset. I just wish you would say what you have to say Eric."

"Look Sheila, I don't have anything to say, except I've been focusing on my schoolwork lately. It's very important to me."

"Are you sure that's all?"

Damn, she was jealous. That was cool though. At least I knew I had a sure *piece*.

"Just chill-out Sheila, before you go too far."

"Are you threatening me?"

"No. I'm just saying relax."

She smacked her lips and walked off. What was her problem? Oh well, I was back on the register, but this time I was training Cyndi. "O.K., Cyndi, this is the register...."

"Do you like Kim?"

Oh no, not this again. I immediately looked over to the fries where Kim was working. I caught her looking, but she didn't think I did. I knew she was listening, so I played.

"Yeah girl...! Kim is so fine, I can't get her out of my mind!" Kim raised her head, but Cyndi spoke.

"Really?"

"SYKE!" I laughed. Sometimes I cracked myself up. "Look Cyndi, I like both of you guys, but just as friends. That's all, friends, o.k.?"

"Oh well that's cool, 'cause me and you wouldn't look right anyhow." Cyndi distastefully mumbled.

"Excuse me?"

"Well, you know."

"No, I don't Cyndi. What are you saying?"

"Well, 'cause I'm light-skinned and you black."

"Say what?" I asked, completely ignoring my customer outside.

"How would that look?" she continued. "I mean, I'd just rather go with somebody my own color." She was serious too! Man, this day was messed up! First, I got to school late and get detention for it. Then, *Yolana the ball-breaker* attacks! Then Sheila cops an attitude with me for no reason. And to top it all off, I was standing in the middle of the South with a brainwashed high yella' half- pint segregating me! I just stared at Cyndi for a moment, waiting for her ignorance to dawn on her. She had no clue.

"Look Cyndi, you're young and I like you, so I'm gonna let that slide. But the next time you say something that stupid to me..."

I stopped myself because I knew I couldn't change her heart. Someone had brainwashed her. So I just turned my back to her. I didn't know how or why, but that little girl had just hurt me. She apologized later, out of guilt I guess. It didn't matter though, the damage was done. Man, so many people think the same way. Somebody must've told her she was pretty because of her light complexion. I was so tired of that. Everywhere I went it was the same old bull. Everytime I heard brothers talkin' about a fly girl, she's light-skinned. If she wasn't, then she had to be dressed to show her other *assets*. All of our music videos... light-skinned girls with long hair. I almost quit watching "Soul Train!" I was in the drugstore one night getting some shampoo and I was checking in the 'black folk' section. I noticed that all but one face on our products were light complexioned. People be trippin'! I've even heard of people marrying certain people just so the children could look a certain way. I don't know who came up with the concept that one skin tone was better than another was, but they're way off! It seemed like the lighter you were, the more attractive you were. When in essence, it's all yet another comparison to white people. That's why so many of them try to get with us. They did that in slavery times, now it's legal. Then it's like, "Oh yes, Leroy and I are so happy!" **YEAH RIGHT!** Brotha's wanted to try that pink so they can feel like the **man**. Just like white women wanted that big ass hershey bar they thought we all had in our pants. Well, I wasn't going for the 'Okey-doke'! I always thought sisters were fly. I mean, I'm all for people loving each other truthfully... if it's truthful. That's sweet. We were all the time claiming some form of Black Power. Then we separate our *own* selves. The more I thought about it, the more I wanted to choke Cyndi. All my life I had to endure black jokes and cracks. Like, "You so black, you sweat coffee!" Or, "You so black, your shadow looks for *you*!" I heard millions of them. Although some of them were funny, I never really understood why my own people would say them to me. Like I was the lowest class of black because I was darker. Which meant I was ugly. Which meant I was stupid. Which meant I was poor. Which meant I was violent. Which meant I wanted that white woman's purse. Which meant I was a thief. Which meant people should be afraid of me. Which meant I couldn't be trusted. Which meant I was despised, by black and white people. Which meant conclusively... I was screwed. I'm so glad Mama always taught me to respect myself, protect myself, and love me for me. That way I could overlook ignorance.

9:00p.m. Finally. I'd been on that register forever it seemed. It was definitely time to go. On my way to the clock, I saw Kim sitting in the office looking into space.

"Hey what's the matter shorty?"

"Nothing."

"Oh come on, you can tell me."

"It's o.k." She was being evasive, so I got serious.

"Kim, what's the problem?"

" O.K., my mama's car broke down again, and now me and Cyn' gotta wait till the store closes so Maurice can take us home. I was gonna call us a cab, but we aint got but four dollars put together." She looked so pitiful. I couldn't stand it.

"Don't sweat it Kim, I'll take you home."

"You will?"

"Yeah sure, now call your mom back and tell her you're on your way."

"Hey thanks Eric!" As I punched out, I overheard Kim breaking the good news to Cyndi. I didn't bother changing clothes because I was tired.

"Let's go ladies." Cyndi just *had* to say something.

"You're gonna take us for real?"

"Yeah Cyndi, that is, unless I'm not *light* enough to drive you." She rolled her eyes to heaven. I hoped she got the point. When we got to my car Cyndi immediately hopped to the backseat and said,

"Yo man, you got any music?"

"Yeah girl."

"Wha'cha got?"

I went down my list. She wasn't impressed. Kim was staring out the window, into space again.

"A penny for your thoughts?" I asked.

"Huh?"

"I'll give you a penny for what you're thinking."

"That's o.k."

"How about a quarter?"

"Naw man, Cyndi blurted, she's thinking about Warren!"

"No I'm not Cyndi, so why don't you just shut up!"

"Don't get mad at me 'cause he dumped yo' ass."

"Screw you Cyndi!"

"Screw *you*, 'ho!"

I couldn't believe the mouths on these kids.

"Hey! If you two are gonna fight, you're not gonna do it in my car, because I don't recall either of you making a payment!" There was a long pause. " That sounded pretty corny didn't it?"

Then we all said "yep yep" like GUY, and cracked up.

"So where do you guys live?"

"In the woods." Cyndi proudly stated.

"What?"

"In Sherwood Oaks." Kim clarified.

"Oh really?" I asked.

"Yeah, what's wrong?"

"Oh, nothing." Nothing hell, I had heard that Sherwood Oaks made Compton look like a circus! Anyway, I swallowed my heart and drove on.

"O.K., make a left right here." Cyndi instructed. " See that house right there?"

"The white one?" I asked.

"Naw, the blue one beside it."

"Yeah, I see it."

"That's my house."

I kept driving.

"So?"

"So stop!"

"When, now?"

"Why you playing Eric?"

"Alright, alright."

I drove back to her house. As she got out, she mumbled thanks. I couldn't believe my ears. Cyndi? Grateful?

"No sweat shorty."

I thought Kim was getting out also, but didn't. Cyndi told Kim to call her and then they did that hi-five and a snap thing that Tisha always did. Girls.

"O.K., now I live down the street and to the left."

I honked my horn as we drove off. Cyndi turned back and waved. Kim smiled.

"She's your best friend isn't she?"

"Yeah, Cyn's my girl. She just gets on my nerves sometimes."

"Can I ask you a personal question Kim?"

I saw her preparing herself.

"O.K."

"Why did you get so upset when Cyndi mentioned that dude's name?"

"Who? Warren?"

"Yeah, Warren."

"He aint nobody."

"He must be *somebody* for you to snap like that."

"Oh, I just got mad because Cyndi's mouth is too big. She don't think, she just talks."

"True."

"That's all. There's my house right there."

"You're not gonna answer my question are you?"

"Wha'cha talkin' about?"

I drove an extra block and parked.

"Yo Kim, I'm trying to reach out to you, and you're trying to push me away. How come?"

"I'm not trying to push you away."

"Then what's wrong? I told you I didn't want anything from you. Is it because I'm too dark?"

"No. I don't think like that." (Cool.)

"Then what's up?"

"I don't know. I'm just not used to no guy tryin' to be my friend."

"Yeah well, some guys need friends too Kim."

"Alright, here goes. Warren, my ex-boyfriend broke up with me because I didn't want to do it with him.

She looked embarrassed and shocked that she told me that.

"You mean have sex with him?"

She shrugged her shoulders.

"You liked him too, didn't you?"

"Yeah."

I didn't know why, but that bothered me.

"Damn Kim, do you want me to beat him up for you?"

"That's o.k."

It was a joke, but it looked like she was considering it!

"Listen Kim, I know it hurts when people do you like that. But you gotta put them out of your mind and go to the next beat."

"I'm trying."

"What I wanna say is, I know it's hard to trust guys after that punk, but I wanna be different. I want to be your friend. I'm asking if we can be friends. That's all. Would you be my buddy? Please?"

"O.K."

For the next week or so we went to the movies and everything. She insisted on Cynthia joining us everytime. Which was cool with me. That way I could get to know both of them. They were both 14, and freshmen at Bradley High, across town. They were really down to earth kids. One Friday, I took them to see "Coming to America", with Eddie Murphy. When we walked in, the guy that took our tickets almost got smacked. Talkin' 'bout "Yo homie, which one of'em is yours?" I was like, "Both of'em!" and put my arms around them. He mumbled something behind us, but I ignored him. We had a good time anyway. On the way back I popped in my new cassette, "The Gyrlz". The first song on the tape was there #1 hit, and my personal favorite, It's Over. When it came on, Cyndi jumped up.

"Ooh ooh! That's my song!"

"O.K. then, I said, I'll be the first verse. Cyn, you be second. Kim you come in with the harmonies."

We sang the mess out of that song! Ever since then, I had a new name for my two friends. The Gyrlz*.

We sang that that song everytime we got together. Even without the music behind us. I went to work singing.

One day, some *igit* mopped the dining room floor. Whoever it was didn't know jack about mop water, because I could smell the bleach from all the way in the kitchen. Which meant the floor was slippery. I was taking an order, when Kim walked by and smiled. I winked at her. She was carrying the ketchup pump to the dining room. It was almost as big as she was. With her little self. "Drive to the window please." I so patiently asked my customer. That's when I heard it. **CRASH!**What was that? I thought. When I turned around, I saw the entire front line laughing and pointing to the dining room.

(Oh no, Kim!)

I left my customer and dashed to the front. Kim was on the floor holding her arm. Ketchup was all over the place. Even Sheila was laughing. I exploded.

"What the hell is so funny?!!!"

I ran over and picked her up. "Come on shorty, I've got you." She had ketchup all over her. I wiped her face with my shirt and took her to the bathroom to help her wash it off.

"Are you o.k.?"

"Yeah." she replied, with a broken smile. "But I bumped my elbow."

"Well, better that than your face, however, if you had pickles, you could be a burger."

We laughed it off. Together. She was still upset, but not like I was. I stormed back over to my register. The customer looked like he was running out of patience. I was waiting for him to say something smart. I would've put his food on the hood of his car... out of the bag. And here came Sheila's happy ass.

"What's wrong with you Eric?"

"What's wrong with *you?*"

"So she busted her butt. Damn. What's the biggie? I thought it was funny so I laughed. Don't make a big deal out of it o.k.?"

"Get away from me Sheila."

"Do what?"

"I know I didn't stutter, now get away from me." I snapped.

"Oh, it's like that?"

"Yeah, just like that!"

"Fine, Eric. At least now I know what you've been so busy *focusing* on!"

If we were in the movies, I would've given her one of those Hollywood slaps. She walked away anyway, luckily. When Kim came back in, she heard snickers and tamed laughter from the crew. She was embarrassed. It showed all over her face. Sheila was smirking intentionally. (Oh how she'd pay!) Cyndi gave Kim a hug and they cracked up. Everybody else joined in because they couldn't hold it anyway. I still didn't feel like laughing. The thought that my little buddy was hurt bothered me. She saw me frowning.

"It's o.k. Eric, I'm alright." she smiled.

"Yeah, I can see that." I said, trying to smile with her.

"Thanks."

"Anytime kiddo."

I drove the Gyrlz home that night. Of course we sang our song. That time without the music. That's when I noticed it. Cyndi could sing. I mean really *sang!*

"Yo hold up, hold up! Cyndi, sing by yourself for a minute."

"Uh-oh, a solo!" she exclaimed.

Then homegirl blew.

"I always doubted/ that you loved me / for you used the words I love you / so carelessly."

"She can sing can't she?" Kim stated, promoting her friend.

"Word up!" I couldn't believe that girl. "Hey girl, you need to be on "Showtime at the Apollo" or something with that voice."

"I already told her."

She was still singing when she got out of the car. Even when we drove off! She looked like she had found a new toy. When we got to Kim's house, she reached over and hugged me.

"What was that for?"

"Well, I couldn't thank you in front of Cyn'. She already thinks we're talkin'. So thanks man."

"Hey, I gotta look out for my little sister right?"

"That's right." We were really getting close. And I liked that. It made me feel... I guess.... responsible. Me, a big brother and stuff. Man I was ettin' soft in my old age.

Chapter 8:

Sweet As Can Be

THE NEXT DAY WAS the bomb from the beginning! I could smell it in the air from the moment I awoke. It was April 12, 1989. Now to the average Joe, that date meant maybe nothin'. However, that day was my birthday! I was 18 years old. As soon as I got up, I dashed to the bathroom to count my beard hairs. When I got back to my room, Ma had slipped a card on my bed. She must've known how long I would be in the bathroom. It was beautiful.

Son, from the first day I saw you
I knew you would be,
The most beautiful light and reflection of me.
Your love and friendship
Means the world to me,
I wish you love eternally.
As you grow on this earth
You'll only get better,
As the words of my heart are here on this letter.
I give God the praise
For what He has done,
In granting you, Eric, to me as a son.

Happy Birthday, Mama.

Ma was the only person who could make me cry.

"So what do you wanna do tonight Birthday boy?" She asked.

"Let's go to the movies Ma."

I was always one who enjoyed the simple things.

SAT reports came out the following week. I was shaking when I finally got mine. I mean, when your future is about to be dropped in front of your desk, it kinda does something to you. As soon as it hit the desk I grabbed it. Everyone ripped their's right open. I got scared.

"Go ahead man." this guy named Wilbert, said. I asked what he got. " I don't know man, it just says 74.823 %."

"Well what does the test percentage say?"

"Oh here it is, 75%. I passed!" He yelled.

The whole class looked at him like, "sit down fool."

"Yo Eric, open yours man!"

"Naw, that's alright." I said.

"Aw c'mon man," Wilbert insisted, "you smarter than me, so I *know* you passed."

So I opened it. 88%. (Yes!) I yelled too. I didn't even care. I barely heard my other classmate's responses.

"Yep yep!"

"Cool!"

"Dang!"

I couldn't wait to show Mama. When I got home I took one of the pictures off the wall and put my test result in the frame. I knew she would spot it. Mama didn't miss nothin'! The phone rang.

"Hello?"

"Hello Eric, it's me."

It was Sheila. I hung up in her face. I knew she'd call back, so I answered the phone with ... "What?"

She knew I was still mad at her, so she kept her tone down.

"Eric, we need to talk."

"Talk about what?"

"About us."

"What us?"

"May I come over?"

"I don't care."

"Then I'm on my way."

I just hung up after that. Next thing I knew, she was knocking on my door.

"Can I help you?"

"Can I come in?" she sharply retaliated.

I didn't wanna act immature, so I let her slide with that one. She came in with a white cut-off blouse and some stonewashed Levi's. Now was it me, or did stonewashed jeans make everybody's ass look right? Well her's sure did. But I was still mad so we skipped the formalities.

"Why'd you try to diss me at work Eric?"

"I didn't, but I should've."

"Why, because of Kim?"

"Well......yeah.....I mean no. I.... I mean, I don't have to explain her to you."

"Why not?"

"Because she's my business."

"Your business."

"Yeah. Just like Mike is **your** business."

"That's not fair Eric?"

"Fair? What's not fair is the fact that you come over here and get sexed and then go back home and get screwed again!"

She slapped me.

"Damn you Eric!"

Man, those guys on TV must've been hard as hell, because I was about to cry. That stung like a mob!

"Get out Sheila."

"What?"

"I said get out!"

"I'm sorry Eric."

"Yeah, you sure are sorry."

"So it's like that?"

"That's how you made it Sheila, so that's how it is."

"So can I call you?"

"Sure, fine."

I just wanted her out of my sight. When she left, I couldn't think of anything but spiting her. So I called Monica. I wanted to take her out, but she said she'd cook for me. Nobody ever did that but Ma. So as soon as Moms got home, I told her I was going to hang with Tyrone. I knew she wouldn't check up on me because she couldn't stand Tyrone's mother. "That woman talks too much." Ma would always say. So I jetted on down to Monica's. I wondered what she'd have on this time. What kind of music? What colors? Man, I couldn't wait to touch her, to feel her. I imagined us doing it all the way there. By the time I parked, my fly was open. I didn't touch nothin' though. I wasn't no fag man. I rang her doorbell in eager anticipation. But when she opened the door, it was something totally different. She had a regular Oxford shirt with regular jeans. She looked like a regular person! What happened to my sex goddess? She looked as though she'd been crying.

"Hello."

"Hi."

"Come on in."

I went in and sat on the sofa. She went to the kitchen. I felt so odd just sitting there, so I called to her from the livingroom.

"So....... what've you been up to Monica?"

"Oh, nothing much."

"What'cha cooking?"

"You'll see in a sec'."

Whatever it was, it sure smelled good. She brought it out in a big plate and sat it on the table. Then she signaled for me to come over.

"Do me a favor."

"Sure."

"Get the wine from the freezer."

Get the what? I had never tasted wine before. Nonetheless, I kept my mouth shut and pulled the dark bottle out of her freezer. It had a cork in it and everything. She pulled these two tall glasses from the cupboard and sat them at both ends of the table.

"Would you like to pour the wine?"

Yeah right. I could just picture myself screwing it up. So I just popped the cork and handed her the bottle. We ate her famous lasagna. It was delicious. It took all I had not to spit out that wine, but I handled it.

"So Monica, what's on your mind?"

"Nothing in particular." she quickly responded.

"It has to be something in order for you to have cried."

"My eyes look that bad huh?"

"Yes."

"Tell me this Eric. Why is it that when you do your best to help someone or make them happy, they always jerk you?"

Now what was I supposed to say to that? (" Gee Monica, I wouldn't know because I'm screwing two other women besides you.")

"I'm not sure Monica. However, you mustn't dwell on whomever it was, because there may be someone out there who would do you right and you'd just pass him by."

She smiled, because I was pointing to myself the whole time. I scooted my seat beside hers and kissed her on the cheek.

"There, now isn't that better?"

"Better."

She took me over to the couch and laid me down. Then she took her shoes off and laid in front of me. I put my arm around her and we............watched television.

Man, my senior year was flying! We went through the annual "College Day". I spoke with a rep. from USC, one from NCCU, and even one from Harvard, just for the heck of it. The representative looked at me like "Negro Please!" I could've gone there if I wanted. Luckily for him, law wasn't my thing. Actually, I wanted to go to UNC-Chapel Hill, in North Carolina so I could play basketball. Then I'd be drafted to the Chicago Bulls so I could help Michael out.

But as far as I knew, if your G.P.A. was less than 4.0, or your parents didn't own a bank, you could forget it. So I applied to USC and waited to hear from them by mail.

.

Chapter 9:

The Magic of Romance

Big news! The senior prom was coming up in three weeks. I was psyched! I started saving all my money for my tuxedo. I knew exactly which one I wanted too. It was this fly white tux with a white cummerbund. I set my stuff up in advance. So in three weeks, I would be the man! There was only one thing missing...a date. Suddenly three weeks seemed like three days. Who? Couldn't take Monica, she's too old. Couldn't take Sheila, she was my boss. Plus I wasn't gonna be lookin' over my shoulder all night for Mike. What about Yolana? Yeah.... well, I don't know. I didn't want no corniness. Scratch Yolana. So I pulled out the old *black book*. We all had one.

Hmmm.......now let's see. Angela; too serious. Brandy; too protective. Cheryl; too stupid. Dana; too pregnant. Elaine; too ugly. Damn man, my black book wasn't worth two cents! All them "CREEK BAMMAS" in there. I couldn't think of anybody. Screw it, I'd just go stag. Hell naw, might as well just ask Yolana. I forgot her number, so I went back to flippin' the pages. I accidentally stopped on the "K" section. There were only two numbers there. One was Kmart, and the other was............ Kim! My little buddy from work. Wait a minute, she was only in the 9th grade. I didn't care. I wanted someone special, and that was definitely her. I didn't call her because I was too excited. I couldn't wait to ask her! I practiced in my head at least a thousand times. I saw her at work later on that week. Maurice purposely separated our schedules, because we were having fun I guess. Man, I sure wish I didn't turn into a butt-head like him when I grew up. After we got off that night, I told Kim I needed to ask her something. Cyndi was right in my face too.

"Could you excuse us for a moment Cyndi?"

"I could."

"Well, would you?"

"I would, but......."

"But is right, so but out. AB<u>C</u> ya'!"

I liked talkin' trash with Cyndi. She always had some smart answer for everything. It's a wonder she wasn't child abused. I sat Kim down in the dining room and got us an order of large fries to share.

"What's up?"

"Well Kim, it's like this, I like you a lot. You're very special and a good friend, and..... I'd be honored if you'd be my date to my senior prom."

I closed my eyes. I didn't know what to expect.

"Are you serious?!"

"Yeah girl."

"Man, that would be fresh! Oh wow! For real man? You aint playin' are you?"

"Nope." I replied with the utmost confidence. "Would you like to go?"

"Oh I'd love to!" She was like a kid at Christmas. "Wow man, thanks for asking me. I can't wait to tell mama! Yo Cyn', c'mere girl!"

"Hey, calm down shorty." I tried to restrain her.

Cyndi drug herself over.

"Guess what girlfriend?"

"What?"

"Eric just asked me to go to his senior prom with him!"

Kim was grinning from ear to ear. Cyndi dropped her expression and coldly shrugged her shoulders.

"So what?"

Then she walked off.

"Dag, what's wrong with her?" I asked.

Kim wasn't even fazed.

"When is it Eric?"

"In two weeks."

"Where? What time? What should I wear?"

I had regained my cool by then.

"Wear something white."

Man, she was more excited than I was! Tisha called.

"Hey boy."

"Hey girl."

"I haven't heard from you lately."

"Oh, I've just been chillin' out Tish'."

"Yo, you goin' to the prom?"

"Yeah girl! Crazy?"

"I can't go."

"Why not?" I knew what she was going to say.

"Ma grounded me again."

"Damn Tish', you stay grounded. What for this time?"

"She caught me on my bed with this guy named Delvin."

"Naked?"

"No fool! But still."

"What did Aunt Jean do to him?"

"Nothing."

"Nothing?"

"Naw. He jumped out my window and busted his ankle."

"That's messed up "T". I feel for you."

"Then why you laughin'?"

"I'm sorry, that was funny."

"I didn't find it funny."

I bet she didn't. Aunt Jean would've had her laughing to <u>death!</u>

"I'm sorry."

"Anyway, who you goin' to the prom with?"

"A friend."

"Yolana?"

"Naw!"

"Then who?"

"A friend from work."

"What's her name?"

"Kim."

"Kim what, boy?"

"Her name is Kimberly Nelson."

"Well, excuse me. How old is she."

"Fourteen."

"Fourteen!?"

"Yeah, but she aint stupid or nothin'."

"You like her?"

"Let's just say she's special."

"Well I hope she's cute at least."

"She is, but not as cute as you." I could see her teeth right through the phone.

"I aint cute boy. I'm S-S-S-EXY!"

"Ha!"

"That's right."

"Anyway, I gots to go cuz'."

"Alright. I'll call you later."

"Bye boy."

"Bye girl."

That girl was so crazy. She'd be lucky to even get to a reunion prom! All week, I couldn't think of anything but the prom. I cleaned my car everyday that week. I wanted perfection. I went and got my tux out. I even rented white shoes to match it. Ma and I went shopping for Kim's corsage. We finally decided on a violet. We also bought a separate violet for my jacket. That way Kim and I would both be decked out in white with a little purple for passion. I even bought purple socks in Kmart. And wouldn't you know it? I even found some purple underwear! Kim would never see them, but I would know. Man, my suit was so clean; I could've played Mr. Rorke on Fantasy Island. I wondered what Kim's dress looked like.

Friday afternoon. The prom was Saturday night, 7:00p.m. at the Sheraton Hotel. The school really went all out that year. I saw Kim at work.

"Hiya doll!"

She wasn't herself.

"Hey."

"Oh lord, what's the matter?" She hung her head. "What's wrong shorty?"

"Tell him Kim!" Cyndi blurted out.

At that, Kim ran to the bathroom crying. Cyndi smirked as though she was pleased.

"Kim can't go to your prom."

"Why not?"

She started giggling. "Because her mama can't afford to get her no dress!"

Some of the girls on line overheard and laughed with her.

"Y'know Cyndi, for somebody's best friend, you aint shit!"

"Oohs" came from everyone. She dropped her smile. I was just waiting for a smart response so I could throw her little ass in the french-fry bin! When Kim came back in, she didn't even look at me. I understood. Money was tight. It always seemed like it was with blackfolk. When I was younger, Mama had to work two jobs. I promised her that as soon as I grew up, I would buy her a house and take care of her. She would always brag to the neighbors of how proud she was of me. Ma. That night I called Kim's house. Her mother answered.

"Is this Eric?"

"Yes mam it is."

"Look sugar, I'm sorry about Kimmy, but I just can't afford it this month.

"That's alright Ms. Nelson."

"I know it meant a lot to you too son."

"Well. Why can't she go in another dress?" I asked.

"Child, she don't wanna wear none of her mama's dresses. She wants this white dress in the window at the mall. That dress costs at least $75.00 that I sho' don't have! She was tellin' it all. "By the way, how's your Mother?"

"She's good."

"Well that's good. Tell her I said hello."

"Yes mam."

"Well, goodnight son."

"Wait Ms. Nelson!"

"Yes?"

"Do you remember the exact dress she wanted?"

"Sure. It's the smallest white one in the window. How come?"

"I don't know, just in case."

"Well, Lord help you, 'cause I done ran out of cases!"

We laughed.

"Goodnight Eric."

Kim's mom was cool. She wasn't that bright, but she sure loved her "Kimmy". Just like my Mama. Always looking out for me and my best interests. Moms. When I hung up, I knew what had to be done. How to do it was the question.

Saturday morning. Prom Day. I knew Kim was off work, so I called her.

"Hello?"

"Hey shorty!"

"Eric?" She sounded surprised to hear from me.

"Yep yep."

"I-I'm sorry...."

"Oh girl hush. Listen, what are you doing today?"

"Nothing."

"Good, then you're coming with me."

"Where?"

"Well since we can't go to the prom, I thought we'd just hang out."

"O.K. You want me to call Cyn'?"

"Nope. It's just me and you today."

"O.K. what time?"

"Now."

"Now?"

"Now. I'll be there in ten minutes."

"Take your time."

"See ya!"

I called Tisha.

"What's up?"

"I need a big favor 'T'."

"What?"

"Remember Kim, the girl I told you about?"

"Yeah?"

"I need you to fix her hair for the prom."

"Say what?"

"Oh come on Tisha, you know how good you are with hair."

She was more than good. Tisha needed her own salon. She could do it all from crimps to curls to perms. She even hooked up Ma once. Yep. That was my baby cuz'.

"Eric. I barely have enough stuff for my own head."

"I'll get you some more stuff, I promise."

"Promise my butt boy, you gonna pay for this."

"Thanks 'T', I love you."

"Yeah yeah. When?"

"In a half hour."

"A half hour?!"

"Oh this is **really** gonna cost."

"I'll see you in a few."

"O.K."

When I got to Kim's house, I beeped my horn twice. She came out running with her little Duke University cap on. Her mother waved from the window. I waved back.

"Man, that was quick." Kim panted. "Where are we going?"

"You'll see."

"Tisha, this is Kim. Kim, this is my cousin Tisha."

"I like your hair." Kim said.

"Thank you girl."

"Who did it for you?"

"I did."

"You did?"

"Yeah girl. I could do yours if you'd like."

"For real?"

"Sure."

Oh smack! Tisha was almost as smooth as her big cousin. Kim was falling right into it too.

"Let me see your hair."

Kim took her cap off. Her hair looked like a bike sprocket! I couldn't help but laugh.

"Shut up Eric." they both said.

"C'mon girl, I can hook you up real quick."

"But me and Eric...."

"Don't worry," I interjected. " I'll go and get us some food."

"Get me a burger."

"Me too, and a shake."

"Cool."

Kim waved good-bye. I winked at her. If only she had a clue.

I went to the bank teller machine up the street and took out $150.00 of my college savings. Dad would slip me some cash on occasion and I deposited every dime. It's true; a little bit *does* add up to a lot. Ma would kill me otherwise. I hoped she would understand. I mean, a guy's senior prom only happens once in his life. I went straight to the mall. I knew there was only one store that sold prom dresses, so it was easy to find.

"Excuse me Miss?"

"Yes?"

"I'm looking for a white prom dress."

"Could you be a little more specific?"

"Umm...yeah! It's the smallest one you have.... and you had it in the window."

"Oh, you mean the Victorian gown. I'll take a look for you."

"Thanks."

She saw that I was in a hurry, so she ignored this other customer. (Well alright!) It was about time. When she came back out, she had this gorgeous little gown in her arms. I wasn't sure though, that thing looked like it costed more like $750.00.

"Umm.... how much does that dress cost?"

"It's on sale for $75.00."

"Yes!....oh excuse me."

"My, you're exited."

"Yes mam I am."

She even gift-wrapped it in a white box with a purple ribbon! This was too much. Shoes! She needed shoes! I ran right into the nearest Payless Shoes.

"Excuse me sir, I need a pair of white heels please."

He looked at me like, 'What the hell?'.

(Man, just get the damn shoes!) I thought.

"Wha-what size sir?"

"Oh, well she's about this tall and umm.... wait a second."

I darted out and called Tish' for the info. She told me she wears a size 5, and that she wished she could go to my prom.

"You didn't tell her anything did you?"

"Eric, just because I'm beautiful, that doesn't make me stupid."

"Thanks cuzzy. I'm on my way back."

"Bye boy."

"Yes sir, she wears a size 5. Do you have them?"

"One moment."

He found them. Yes!

"That will be $12.25."

That's all? Man, girl's shoes were cheap. I grabbed those babies and headed straight for Kim's house. I knocked. Her mom came to the door.

"Well hello Eric. Where's Kimmy?"

"She's getting her hair done."

"She's what?" She gasped in amazement.

"Yes mam, and these are for her."

"B-b-but how?...Uh..why?" She sounded just like Kim.

"May I put these in her room?"

"You sho' can. Come on in here baby!"

I laid the boxes on her bed with a small card attached saying, "C U at 7." Her mother was speechless. I told her that Kim would be home soon, and asked her to please play along. As I was leaving, she stopped me.

"Bless you son, hear me?"

"Yes mam, thank you."

On my way back to the car, guess who I ran into? Cyndi. Dang! I knew I couldn't avoid her so...

"Hi Cyndi. How are you?"

"Fine. What was in those boxes?"

Oh boy, here we go.

"What boxes?"

"Don't play dumb. Those two white boxes."

"Oh those. That was nothing. Just a present."

"It *aint* Christmas, and it *aint* her birthday either."

"So what?"

"You bought her that dress didn't you?" She rolled her eyes in disgust. "What'chu do that for?"

"Because she deserves it."

"Hmph......she don't love you."

"I didn't ask her to love me. I just asked her to be my date tonight. What's your problem Cyndi?"

"I aint got no problem!"

"Yes you do, and I'll tell you what it is......."

"I said I don't..."

"Your problem is that you're used to getting more attention than Kim. Somebody told you that you were cute because you're light-skinned. So you think you're special. Well, that crap doesn't faze me in the least." She folded her arms and sighed. "And furthermore, I don't care if you don't like it. For the last couple of weeks, you've been dissin' Kim like you don't even know her. And don't think she hasn't noticed. You are no better than she is Cyndi. So despite how many little boys talk to you instead of her, she's still your best friend. She needs you, just like you need her. Now I'm taking her to that prom. Not because of your smart-ass attitude, and not because I want anything from her, but because I like her....as a friend. Are you jealous of her?"

"Hell naw!"

(Damn. Must've struck a nerve.)

"Look Cyn, just be a friend to her, that is if she really *is* your friend. Alright 'shorty bop-bop'?"

Finally, a smile.

"O.K."

"Now gimme a hug girl." I hoped something would stay between her ears. "Well I gotta jet, so I'll see you later Cyndi."

"See ya."

She just stared as I drove off. I flew to get the food and back to Tisha's house. Kim had rollers in hair. I peeked at my watch. It was 1:30p.m. Time was flying! Then I jumped up to use Tisha's phone.

"I gotta check my answering machine." As Tisha started wrapping her hair, I started my act. " Kim, your mom was on my answering machine. She said you gotta come home now!"

"Wha-I'll call her."

"She said it was an emergency, let's go!"

"But I still got these rollers in my hair."

Tish' came right in on time.

"Oh don't worry about'em girl. Just make sure to take them out in an hour."

"O.K."

As Kim rushed to gather her stuff, I slipped Tisha a twenty and kissed her forehead. Then we were out. By the time we got to her house, she still hadn't caught on.

"Well, I'll see you later shorty."

"O.K. Eric."

She jumped out of the car and raced inside. I drove two feet away and waited. 3...2...1...

"OH MY GOD!!" Got her.

After I got dressed, Ma took more pictures than LIFE magazine! I was tryin' not to get an attitude, 'cause I knew this was special to her. Besides, she had to run out of film sometime. Or so I thought.

"How do I look Ma?"

She had that 'Bill Cosby-pudding pop' look on her face.

"Like my baby!"

She pinned my violet on me and handed me Kim's corsage.

"Make sure to drop back by so I can see you two." she said.

"Yes mam."

I kissed her as I headed towards the door.

"Oh yeah, Ma?"

"Yeah baby?"

"Thanks."

"For what?"

"Everything."

She smiled and winked at me. I put a towel over my seat so I wouldn't get a speck of dirt on me. Ma took a picture of me driving off. I turned on the radio. They were kickin' "Kiss", by Prince. That was a talented little dude. I got to Kim's house at exactly 6:59p.m. When I got out, it seemed like her entire block came out to see. Nosey folk! Being I was in the spotlight and all, I took my sweet time getting to her door. Man, I felt cooler than Big Daddy Kane! When I rang the doorbell, I could hear her mother telling the other kids to shut up. She opened the door slowly.

"Woo-wee, just look at you! Turn around!"

She was worse than Ma was.

"Hello Ms. Nelson, is Kim ready?"

"Wait here, I'll get her." She took one step... "KIM?!!, C'mon girl. Don't you keep this good lookin' young man waitin' for you." "Now where in the world did I put my camera?"

Oh no. I ran, well jogged back to the car for her corsage. Man, her neighbors were up on me so close, that I could've given them all corsages! On my way back, I saw her mother back away from the door. And when I got there, Kim came out. I was usually a guy who talked too much. However, when I saw Kimberly Nelson in front of me that evening, only two words came to me.

"Absolutely beautiful."

That she was.

"Kim? I think I've got a new name for you."

"What's that?"

"Princess."

She blushed.

Her mom found her camera. Dag! So after five million pictures, we walked to the car. All of her neighbors watched. She liked that. I watched the little boys her age staring at her. I could hear them a mile away.

"Yo, who's that dude?"

"Aint that Kim?'

"Yo, she looks good!"

When we got to the car, I opened her door for her. I got in on the other side and looked over to her.

"Kim, for a girl, you're one beautiful lady."

"Lawd-a-mercy, look at you two!" Ma exclaimed. "Eric told me you were cute, but you're a doll!"

"Thank you mam."

It seemed the more that Kim smiled, the cuter she became. She had dimples too, so she just sparkled. Ma pulled me to the side and slipped me $50.

"Treat her right son."

"Thanks Ma!"

"My pleasure."

And we were off to the prom. I put in my Keith Sweat cassette and we sang "Make It Last Forever". I wished it could've.

When we got to the Sheraton, the place was packed. Kim was on the edge of her seat. She'd never experienced this type of stuff. I got out and opened her door for her. As we walked in, we did something we had never done before. We held hands. Something about her little hand in mine made me feel good. Everybody was there. All my boys. Even Tyrone found a date. The DJ was playing some Rod Stewart songs at the time. He had to keep everybody happy I guess. Personally I couldn't dance to that crap, so we sat down at a booth in the corner.

"Would you like something to drink Kim?"

"Yes please."

So I went to get us two punches. On my way back, I saw this guy named Byron trying to talk to Kim. I didn't want to spill our drinks, so I took my time getting over there.

"So what's your name baby?"

"Her name is *Cliff*," I interjected, so why don't you step off!"

"Oh, my bad Eric. I didn't know she was yours."

Like she was a coat or something.

"Yeah, ok Byron, whatever."

"Peace 'E'."

"Peace man."

A simple misunderstanding. Then the DJ put on the "Rock wit'chu" remix by Bobby Brown.

"Would you like to dance?"

"Yes."

I led her on out to the floor. Her little arms were too short to go around my neck, so we reversed the order. It seemed as though we were suspended in space. Then she looked up at me with those soft brown eyes of hers. My knees got weak. I had to pull her close just to keep from staring at her. She felt like a little angel in my arms. When the song ended, we were still dancing. I suggested that we take a walk around.

"Alright, but can I go to the ladies room first?"

"I'll wait for you."

As I waited, Laurette Mills passed by. We had English classes together since the 7th grade.

"Oh Eric, is that you? Lookin' good!"

"Thanks."

"Did you come stag?"

"No Laurette, I have a date."

"Oh really?"

"Yes really. As a matter of fact, here she comes now."

Laurette took one look at Kim and busted out laughing.

"What's so funny?" Kim insisted.

"You better hurry up and get her home before her curfew!" she laughed.

"Well....," Kim immediately responded, "You better hurry up and get home before you turn back into a wolf!"

Oh smack! Kim was fast on the draw! I liked that.

"Come on Kim."

"Who was that Eric, and what was her problem?"

"She's in one my classes. I don't know what her problem is though, and I don't even think she knows."

We walked around the hotel.

"Man, some of the girls at your school are crazy!" Kim said.

"I'll say."

"Guess what they were talking about in the ladies room."

"What?"

"Talkin' about which boy they was gonna do it with."

"Stupid."

We went back and danced some more. I was happy. After they crowned the King and Queen, (a black and a white, as usual), people started leaving. It was only 9 p.m., so went and got in line to take pictures. Man, that line was long! Some of them mobs shouldn't have even been in line with those faces! When it was our turn, the photographer told us that we were cute. The first shot, we held hands. For the second pose, I stood behind her with my arms around her little waist.

"O.K. kids, for your last shot, I need you to kiss."

"Say what?" we said.

"Let's go guys..." he persisted. "There's a line down the hall."

That's when it happened. We didn't even think about it. I pulled her to me and kissed her, like on TV.

"Uh... I meant a little kiss... y'know, a peck....., um, excuse me.......? Hey!"

When we came up for air, the entire room was applauding. I felt dizzy. Kim was star struck also. Plus I had her lipstick all over my face. We had to let another couple go in front of us so we could regroup. We apologized to each other simultaneously. But it was nice. Really nice. When we got back in front of the camera, we couldn't stop smiling. I felt like a kid. After that I asked her if she was hungry.

"A little."

"How about Red Lobster?"

She was impressed.

"O.K.!"

Either that kiss blew her mind, or she didn't get out much. Dag! I had left my wallet back home on my dresser.

"We have to make a quick stop first alright?"

"O.K."

At the house the lights were off and Ma's car was gone. I opened the door, turned on the lights, and almost fell out. Ma had hooked the place up! She had set up the diningroom with her "never-use" china. The table even had champagne glasses. Even candles! (Yeah Ma!) So I went out to the car and brought Kim in with my hand over her eyes. I sat her at the table and lifted my hand.

"Wow!"

"You like?"

"Yeah man! You did all this?"

"Yeah." I said, with my lying self.

Ma left me a note on the fridge. "Eric, I hid your wallet so you would have to come back. That's right, I've still got it! Have a great one son. I'll be at your Aunt Bertha's if you need me. Love Ma."

Man, Ma was no joke! She had cooked us some spaghetti and meatballs. Ma didn't cook regular spaghetti though. She would stand there and actually chop each and every ingredient for her sauce. She would boil her spaghetti, strain it, and then boil it again. Then she worked the meatballs to perfection. She was always a patient cook. Which probably meant she started right after we left. She even put some Welch's wine in the freezer! I poured both of our glasses. Then I jetted to the room to put on Luther. I couldn't find him, so I put on Tony Terry's "Forever Yours".

"I'd like to propose a toast Kim."

"O.K."

I raised my glass and she obliged.

"To the most beautiful date and friend a guy could ask for."

She blushed. I was really having fun with her.

Man, we ate almost the entire pot of spaghetti! We talked about growing up and stuff. She had a lot of memories stored in her little head. I hoped that night would forever be one of them. I lit the candles, hit the lights, and threw in my "Slow Jams" tape. We danced from Prince to Atlantic Starr.

"I'm really sorry about kissing you like that tonight Kim."

"Yeah, I'm sorry to Eric."

"It was nice though."

"Sure was."

I leaned down and kissed her.

"Oops! It happened again!" I said jokingly.

"You so silly Eric."

The next thing I knew, we were swapping tongues. I could tell she didn't know how because she was cleaning my gums! I didn't mind though. She was so precious, so fragile in my arms. I couldn't stop kissing her. I felt happy holding her. However, I felt myself going under. I knew we had to stop. I suddenly pulled myself away from her.

"What's wrong Eric?"

"Nothing. It's just that this isn't right. I mean, I-I mean...we should stop. Y'know what I mean?"

"I think so."

"Cool."

"Cool."

"I've got something for you princess."

"What?" she asked with outstretched arms.

"Close your eyes."

I reached into my pocket and pulled two rings out. I had gotten them from a gumball machine when I was a kid. Every kid has something that he keeps. I turned her hand over and placed one on her ring finger. I was even able to put mine on my pinky.

"Can I open my eyes now?"

"Alright."

She smiled at them.

"What are these for?"

"These are our friendship rings." I replied. "As long as we're buddies, they stay on. Dig?"

"Dug."

I drove her back home. I could see her house lights on a half a mile away. So I stopped the car before we got there.

"Kim, may I have a goodnight kiss now? Because I know your mom aint even playin' that!"

She looked as though she was glad that I asked.

"Well, since this is your prom night, I guess this last one won't hurt."

She closed her eyes and puckered her little lips. So I kissed her. Right on the cheek.

Chapter 10:

Friends

Every day at work we'd touch rings like we were the Wondertwins or something. Cyndi didn't like it. Neither did Sheila. Then here come the rumors. First, we went together, then we were doing it, next thing I knew, she was pregnant by me! Sometimes folk could be so ignorant. One day Mike came to the store to give Sheila her keys and she got all kissy-kissy with him in front of me. Like that was supposed to hurt me. That was alright though, because Monica just so happened to drop by later that day. So I took my lunch break early and went back to her place with her. She only lived about ten minutes away from the job. You'd be amazed at how much you could do in about 40 minutes. I got back one minute late, and there was Sheila.

"You're late Eric."

"Sorry 'bout that."

"I saw you get in that woman's car."

"And?"

She rolled her eyes at me. Hard.

"Alright Eric, play your little games."

"Look Sheila, I came as soon as I could!"

"Yeah, I just bet you did."

I tried to act like I didn't understand, but I did. Damn man, I swore the next time I saw a figure like Sheila's, I would keep right on truckin'! Shoot, some people will own you if you let them. I wasn't *anybody's* slave. I bet if I didn't have anything between my legs, she'd have no use for me. Sheila was seriously on my nerves. On top of that, here came Tammy. Tammy went to college with Sheila for one year, then she dropped out. Oh well, I guess college wasn't for everybody.

"Hey loverboy."

"Hey Tammy."

"What's up with Sheila."

"You tell me." I replied.

"What, she's not talkin' to you either?"

"Nope."

"Well don't worry, we women get like that sometimes."

"I aint stuttin' Sheila." I said defensively. "Just so she don't put me on fries."

"You're so stupid boy."

That was it.

"Boy huh?"

"If only you were older..."she teased.

"Tammy, let me share something with you. My Father taught me something. He said, "Son, when you're young, you got energy, but you don't know how. And when you're old, you know how, but you got no energy. So when you get to the point where you've learned how, and you still got the energy...do it. Do it long, do it hard, do it twice, but make sure you do it good." "Y'know what I'm saying girl?"

"So do you think you learned anything?"

"I think you're afraid to find out if I did or didn't."

"Boy please."

I could see her pride was injured, so I went for blood.

"Hey it's alright Tammy, I can understand you being scared and all..."

"Tammy aint hardly scared O.K.?"

"If you say so."

"Alright then, that's a bet. What time do you come in Saturday?"

"11:30a.m."

"Well I start at noon, so come over my house Saturday at 9 o'clock." she said boldly.

"I don't think so homey."

"Why not?"

"Because you live with Anna."

"She won't even be there. She opens the store on Saturday. So you comin'?"

"Alright Tammy!"

"Alright Eric!"

"Don't be playin'."

"Naw, don't you be playin'."

I got to her house at 8 o'clock. I knew Anna was gone because they shared this little yellow Honda and it was gone. So I drove on up. I rang the doorbell, but she didn't answer. So I knocked. Finally.

"Good morning."

"Good morning." she said in a robe, looking like death warmed over. "I thought we said 9 o'clock, Eric."

"We did, I'm just early."

"Real early."

When I walked in, the place was worse than my room! Damn. I figured with two women, at least it would be clean. Oh well. Tammy still had rollers in her hair.

"Have a seat in the livingroom." she said.

"I would if I could find it."

"Very funny. Let me take a quick shower."

"Need any help?"

"No thanks."

What a diss.

While she was in the shower, her phone rang. Damned if I was gonna pick it up. So I ran to the bathroom to tell her.

"Yo Tammy? Tammy?"

In there singing as hard as she could. Her Patti LaBelle sounded more like Benny Hill! I'm surprised the shower glass didn't break. When I opened the door, she was dancing in the tub. Totally unaware of my presence. Her answering machine picked up the call, so I just stood there watching. She had a nice little body. Almost athletic. I was checking her out from head to toe. I handed her a towel.

"Eric!"

"What?"

"What'chu doing in here?"

"I....uh...got lost."

I was looking her all up and down.

"Have you found what you're lookin' for?"

"I think so. Come over here, I'll dry you off."

When we got to her room, I laid her on her bed, picked up a bottle of baby oil, and began to explore. In my mind I compared her parts to the others I had seen. Hmmm...very interesting. Her pubic hair was straight. Like a white lady's. It was trimmed too. That was neat. It looked good so I went down for a whiff. It was weird, the others smelled kinda like fish, but her's smelled like cranberries. Cool.

"Mind if I have a taste?"

"Oh you know how to do that?"

I smiled.

"You tell me when I finish."

I took it nice and slow, because I had something to prove. I had learned almost everything about sex by watching Dad's old *dirty* tapes. Man, her stuff was sweet. I couldn't stop. Even though she jerked all over the bed trying to make me. She kept on whispering, "Stop!" Man, I couldn't wait to jump those bones. Good thing I wore my rubber over there. When it was over, she was so tired she called into work sick.

When I got to work, Sheila was off. (WHEW!) So was Kim. (Damn.) Nobody was there but Anna, Maurice, and Cyndi. Maurice put me on the grill and out Cyndi right beside me. Great.

"What up shorty?"

"Hey," she dryly responded.

"Long time no talk."

"Yeah, I know, since you been talkin' to Kim." Oh brother, here we go again! "You go with her don't you?"

"No Cyndi. She's my friend. Just like I *thought* you were."

"Then how come you haven't asked me on no date?"

"Because I'm too dark remember?"

"You need to drop that," she said distastefully.

"Dropped. O.K., what time do you get off tonight?"

She looked surprised.

"Six."

"Cool. We'll just pick up Kim and go to a seven o'clock movie."

"Why we gotta get her?"

"Why not?" I asked. "Don't you want your best friend to come?"

"Forget it Eric!"

"Why are you getting mad?"

"I aint mad!"

I saw where she was coming from, so I put on my baby voice.

"Don't wuv me no mo' mommy?"

I knew she couldn't resist.

"Yeah, but you foul."

"Why am I foul?"

"Because you act like you don't wanna go nowhere with me by myself," she pouted.

"Alright. Fine. We're going out tonight then...alone."

I took her to see <u>The Color Purple.</u> It was playing at the $2.00 Cinema. I had already seen it a hundred times. I loved that film. It was just so real. I thought it should've gotten all the awards instead of the rest of those crappy films. Like, what the hell did <u>Out of Africa</u> mean? Two whitefolk falling in love and some elephants! Big deal. And that crap got a lot of awards. We brought food from the job in our booksacks. Soon after the film started, Cyndi began fidgeting.

"What's the matter?"

"I'm cold."

So I gave her my jacket. My favorite part of the movie came then. The part when they sang <u>"God is tryin' to tell you somethin'."</u>

"Yo check it out Cyn'...Cyn'?"

She was knocked out asleep. She must've really been tired. Poor thing. Even fourteen year olds ran out of gas sometime. She looked so peaceful. So much cuter when she wasn't talking. When the film was over, I waited until everyone left to wake her.

"P-s-s-t. Hey shorty. Cyndi?"

"Huh?", she muttered with closed eyes.

"Wake up baby."

"I'm up mama."

I could've just melted. I kissed her forehead.

"Wake up girl."

I had to shake her a bit, but she eventually came to. I had to practically carry her to the car. When she got in, I let her seat back so she could sleep. I woke her up at her house. She apologized for falling asleep.

"No sweat kiddo."

She got out, waved bye-bye, and dragged up the steps. I drove off once I saw she was in the house. I was tired myself. I could barely focus on the road. As soon as I got in, I fell out on my bed. I knew what it was then. Tammy. Boy, sex can really drain you. That's why Tammy called in. Wait a second, then why was Cyndi so tired?!?

"N-a-a-a-a-h."

Sunday morning. I heard Ma's gospel music kickin'! The smell of bacon and pancakes filled the house. Sunday mornings always felt different as opposed to the other days. They felt...I don't know...easy.

"Rise and shine baby. Get ready for church." Mama declared from the kitchen.

Dag! I hated going to church. I mean, I dug the choirs and all, but the service bored me. Oh well, I thought, maybe I'd meet a cutie there. I wore my double-breasted suit. Ma got it for me for Easter. I even put my earring in. I was too clean! When we got there, (late), the Youth Choir was singing 'Amen'. They were good too! Ma tried to get me to join, but I wasn't with it. I didn't feel like I belonged. Like I wasn't good enough to sing for a church. Ma would always say, "You're *not* singing for the church. You're singing for God." Ma always said cool stuff like that. I stared at the choir. Most of them were in my age range. I wondered if they were having sex like I was. I couldn't believe I was sitting in church thinking something so ridiculous. There was a visiting Pastor from Virginia speaking. I didn't catch his name, but I'd never forget that sermon. It was called, "Don't waste your youth."

"Young brothers and sisters don't waste your youth. Give God your energy, give him your talents, and give him your hearts. Don't think that just because you're young nobody understands you. Y'see, the God I serve will give you a peace that passeth all understanding!" (Well.) "Turn with me in your Bibles to first Corinthians chapter seven and verse one." "Now concerning the things whereof ye wrote unto me; It is good for a man not to touch a woman. Nevertheless to avoid fornication let every man have his own wife, and let every wife have her own husband." (Preach on!) "So I urge you youngfolk to preserve yourselves. Avoid the drugs. Avoid the alcohol. Avoid the lying and the stealing. Avoid the sexual contact. Give it all to Jesus, and he can fix it for you. Can I get an amen?" (Amen!) "C'mon y'all, somebody out there knows what I'm talking about. Can I get an amen?"(Ha' mercy!!) "More importantly," he continued, "young folk, if you're gonna be hard-headed and do it anyway, protect yourselves. Y'see disease don't care how good you think you look!" Man, when he said that,

it got real quiet in that mob! "Don't matter who you fool, or how many times you fool them, you aint never gonna fool God!"

Damn, was he talkin' to me or what? I had to get out of there.

"Did you enjoy the service?" Ma asked.

"Yeah, it was pretty cool."

"Cool?"

"Well, you know Ma, nice."

"I see," she said, brushing her thumb against her nails. She always did that when she wanted to know something. I headed for my room to change my clothes. "Eric?"

"Mam?"

"Are you having sex?"

"Ma!"

"Answer my question boy."

"No Ma."

"Are you sure? You wouldn't lie to your mother would you?"

"O.K. Ma, it happened once." I ducked because I just knew she was gonna throw something. Luckily she didn't.

"With who?"

"Ma!"

"Well... you did protect your little self, right?"

(Little?) "Yes mam."

"You better had, 'cause if I hear about you getting anybody pregnant, you're out."

"Thanks Ma."

"Don't get smart boy."

I went to the basketball court. It was deserted, so I practiced my all-star skills. My slam-dunk was getting much better. I still couldn't dunk backwards though. I wanted to do it at least before graduation, which consequently was about two months away. When I returned home, Ma was fast asleep. She always took naps after church. I knew she was asleep when I walked in, because the answering machine had taken a message or two. The first one was Aunt Bertha, talkin' 'bout some cookout. The second one was Yolana talkin' 'bout she missed me and to call her.

"Hello?"

"Hi."

"Well well, if it isn't Mr. No Contact."

"Very funny," I replied, "what's up?"

"Nothin'."

"Nothin'?"

"Not a thing," she reiterated.

"Well, where's the family?"

"They gone shopping."

"I see... and you're all alone."

"Yep."

"I'll be right over."

"O.K."

"Bye."

I wrote Ma a note on her little memo pad and left. I got to Yolana's pretty quickly. She had on black shorts and house slippers.

"So when are they coming back?" I asked.

"Oh they'll be gone awhile. Mama is so slow when she shops."

(Cool.)

"So do you think we can have some fun?"

"What kinda fun Eric?"

I backed her into a wall and lifted her shirt.

"This kind of fun."

"O.K.," she smiled, "but this is all we can do, 'cause I'm on my period."

Damn.

The following Tuesday, we received our Prom pictures. I couldn't wait to open mine. I ripped through the package. I was speechless. Kim was gorgeous! And of course, I was looking rather *fly* myself! Everybody was checking each other's pictures out, so I flaunted mine with the rest of them. I liked the responses I got.

"Y'all look good Eric;" and "Yo man, who's that girl? She's fine."

I couldn't stop looking at them. I picked everything out in them. They were flawless. I couldn't wait to show Kim. I took them to work with me, but she wasn't there. I sat my precious envelope beside my register, and here comes Sheila.

"What's that?"

"These are my prom pictures."

"Ooh let me see!" she said like a kid.

So I gave her the envelope. As she stared at the 8x10, I studied her face for *some* sign of approval or something.

"Well, what'cha think?"

It took her a few seconds to recognize Kim. I could see it in her eyes.

"Well, **you** look handsome."

"Thanks Sheila," I said in amazement.

"Is that the little girl who works here?"

"Yep," I said proudly."

"Why'd you take her?"

"Because I just wanted to. We had a great time. Why?"

"Well......she's so young and all....I mean...look at how short she is. She's barely over your stomach."

"I didn't ask her because of her height Sheila. She was my date, she looked fly, and our the evening was just perfect."

"Yeah, I bet it was."

"See, you get on my nerves with that Sheila!"

"What? I didn't say anything Eric. Besides, whatever you two did is your business."

"You got that right!" I countered.

"I just think she's just a little too young for you, that's all."

"Well maybe **I'm** a little too young for **you** Sheila!"

She walked off as usual. Served her jealous ass right. Always thinkin' somebody's cheating. Well, I was, but I didn't have to answer to her. Poor Mike, I bet that brother couldn't even turn his head in another female's direction without hearing it! I mean, it's one thing for someone to sweat you, but when you feel trapped, that's when there's a problem. With Sheila, it was like sex for ownership. That, I was not havin'!

I clocked Kim's timecard in as soon as I saw her mother's car pull into the parking lot. She and Cyndi came in giggling as usual.

"Hello ladies."

"What up?" Cyndi said to my surprise.

"Oh hey." Kim muttered, like she didn't want to speak.

I grabbed her by her arm until Cyndi went to punch in.

"What'chu mean hey?"

"I gotta go clock in, Eric."

"I already punched you in. Now, what's up with you?"

She looked over her shoulder for Cyndi.

"Cyn' said that you took her to the movies."

"Yeah, she fell asleep though. So what?"

"So...... she said you kissed her. Did you?"

"Kim, I kissed her on her forehead, and that was while she was asleep."

"She said y'all kissed!"

I had never seen Kim that upset. I didn't know how to react.

"Kim, I did not kiss Cyndi on the lips."

"Then why did she say you did?"

"I don't know."

Bad answer. Kim shook her little head in disbelief.

"Eric, I thought you said that you didn't like her like that."

"I don't!" I strained. "Look, I know she's your best friend and all, but she's not telling you the truth. Maybe she's jealous of you and she's just trying to make you mad. I thought that we made a pact Kim. Now you're gonna let a lie separate us? I'm not gonna beg you to believe me, 'cause I know the truth."

"Y-you didn't kiss her?"

"I told you I didn't."

"I believe you."

"You do?"

"Yep."

"Why?"

"Because I know Cyn' be lyin' all the time."

I felt so relieved. Like a ton of bricks was lifted from my neck.

"Thanks for trusting me shorty, 'cause I need my "Princess".

She smiled, so I pulled out our prom pictures and told her to close her eyes. I took her little hand and placed the 5x7 in it.

"Can I open'em now?"

"O.K., open'em."

"Wow!"

"Yeah."

She stared at it for at least a minute.

"Did you get any wallet sized ones?" she asked in awe.

"Yep."

"Could I have one?"

"Sure. You can have that 5x7 too."

"I can?!"

"Well, that is, unless you don't want it."

She snatched it back with the quickness!

"Thanks man! Wait till I show Cyn'- Yo Cyn'!"

"What'chu yellin' for girl? I'm right here."

"Check this out girl!"

Cyndi hesitantly glanced at our photo.

"Yeah, that's nice."

I'd seen more enthusiasm in a walnut!

"Well, how do we look girl?" Kim eagerly continued.

"I like your dress."Cyndi mumbled.

"Yeah, Eric got it for me!"

"I know."

"Look how clean **he** was!"Kim smiled.

"He looked alright."

"Alright?" we both responded.

"Yeah, alright, y'all aint all that!" Cyndi scorned and strutted off.

Well then. We never! I saw where she was coming from so I just let her slide.

"Well I think you looked very handsome." Kim said, overshadowing Cyndi's attitude.

"Thanks babe."

I called her "babe" all loud just to spite Cyndi. It worked too. She turned and rolled her eyes at me. So I blew her a kiss.

Chapter 11:

Signs of Danger

Sheila came over after work. We played cards. Pitty-Pat. I was kicking her butt. Dad *did* teach me how to play cards!

"O.K. son, the first rule to playing this game is never let your opponent think you have a weak hand. Even if you do, giv'em that look like you got a million dollars in the bank! Rule two: Keep your eyes on three things. Their eyes, their hands, and the table. And last but not least son,...never cheat...., that is ..unless you can get away with it."

"O.K. Dad!"

When the game was over, we just stared at each other from across the table. She didn't speak, so I did.

"So... wanna do it?"

"Eric!"

"What?"

"That aint no way to suggest making love!" she snapped.

"But I don't wanna make love, I wanna break you off...hard."

She was obviously disturbed.

"Maybe I should go."

"Why?"

"Because you don't sound like the Eric I know."

"You don't know me anyway," I thought. "I'm sorry Sheila...., would you please love me?" I said with a smirk.

"Real funny." I reached across the table for her hand. "I didn't say yes," she said moving her hand away.

"Aw, come on sexy."

She gave in, and it was back to the bedroom.

As she began taking her clothes off. I pulled up a chair.

"What are you doing?", she asked.

"Just watching."

"Watching what?"

"You."

She stripped to her bra and panties. Damn, her body was so nice! I ripped my clothes off quick-like.

"You wanna help me take the rest off Eric?"

(Hells yes!)

She turned around and pulled her hair up. I came up behind her and began soaking her neck with kisses. Women love that stuff, however, her bra wouldn't unhook. I was just tugging away at it. I kept my eyes closed, that way I could stay in the moment. It wasn't working.

"Damn! Why won't your bra open?"

"Because all of my bras open from the front Eric. Remember?!"

(Busted!) I tried to play it off.

"Yeah, of course I remember. But last time it was from the back."

"No it wasn't!" she snapped. "You must be thinking of some ho'!"

"There aint no ho' but you baby. I-I mean , you the only ho' for me. Damn, I-well you know what I mean."

"Yeah, I know exactly what you mean. Hell with this, I'm going home!"

"Wait Sheila, don't be like that. I just forgot that's all."

"That's bull!"

"For real baby, cross my heart."

"So you're saying that you're not sleeping with anybody else?"

"Yep."

"I hope you're not lying."

"And if I am?"

"If you are, then it's going to come back to you."

She sounded like my Mother.

"Whatever you say Sheila."

I went to pull her panties down, but she did it first. I went to unfasten her bra (the right way), but she did that too. I was beginning to suspect that she had an attitude. So I just sat on the bed and waited. She came over and stood in front of me. I was scared to even put my arms around her waist. She put her's around my neck.

"So.........you still like me?" I asked.

"Maybe."

"Oh it's like that huh?"

"It's how you made it Eric."

With that she forcefully laid me on my back. Then she went down on me. She sucked like mad! It was like she was trying to get gas out of a hose! Then she crawled on top and proceeded to ride me. Not like before though. This time she went real slow and real hard. When I told her I was coming, she jumped off and started stroking me. Three strokes was all it took. She caught it in her hands and rubbed it all over her. (Wow.) Then she started playing with herself! It was like she was performing for me. Then she went back down on me! I was so shocked, because Sheila had never given me head before. She was alright, but she couldn't mess with Monica. If I had to rate them, Monica's head would get the gold. Sheila would get the silver, and Tammy would get the bronze. I wouldn't even let Yolana compete. She'd probably bite my stuff! Some women just can't give head. Some of 'em think they got an ice cream cone, so they're scared to put their lips on it. Then you got the ones that think they're on a microphone, and be spittin' all on your joint. Or else you'll get them mobs that think the got beef jerky, and be gnawing on your jones! Monica knew how to hold it, lick it , squeeze it, and caress it.....man..... I could relax with him in her hands. I wondered what she was doing that night. When Sheila finished she said...

"Now, I bet you'll remember *that*!"

I saw she was trying to act cool. Like she worked me over or something. So I didn't say anything. I just played along.

"That was nice Sheila."

"I know." she responded arrogantly.

Talk about biting your tongue. As soon as she left I went to call Monica. Her answering machine picked up. *"Hi. I'm not in at the moment, but leave me a message and we'll talk. Chow."* (Damn she was smooth!) **Beep!**

"Hi Monica. This is you know who and you know why. Call me when you can. Kisses."

Yeah, now top that. I started cleaning the house because I knew Ma was on the way home. I had it timed perfectly. It took her an average of 23 to 27 minutes, give or take traffic. That way I could do the do and still know when to start cleaning. Ma hated the house dirty. She'd call it names like "Pig-sty"; "Mud-house"; "Dump"; you name it. That's why I put a big fat <u>Do Not Disturb</u> sign on my door. I knew she still went in though. I had to put some cold water and detergent on my sheets because I forgot to put a towel under Sheila. Talkin' 'bout a stain. When that stuff dries, it's a mother to get out. Pun intended.

When Ma pulled up, I was watching the news on channel 5. They were talking about these two boys getting killed. They tried to rob a gas store with B.B. guns. The man behind the counter pulled out a real gun, shot one in the chest and the other in the head. "That was messed up." I thought. Then they showed their pictures. The boys were black. Fifteen and sixteen. The man, 30, white. Come to find out, the boys never pulled their guns out, according to an eyewitness. "They were arguing over some chips or something, then the man just reached down and pulled out a pistol. He shot them before they could run away." They showed the two small body bags at the foot of the counter. That idiot even had the nerve to say that he was afraid for his life. Sure mac. He probably wouldn't even go to court. Still, they shouldn't have been there with guns in the first place. Damn, same ignorance, different time.

Final week. We seniors got our cap and gowns. And we went to the senior picnic at Eastman Beach. What a day that was. I wore my favorite red trunks with green flowers on'em. All the seniors were at that mob! It didn't take me long to find Tyrone. All I had to do was follow the scent of the food.

"What up T?"

"Yo what's up E! It's about time bro. What took you so long?"

"Ma made me do the yards."

"I feel for ya."

"Thanks Tyrone."

"Yo man, have you noticed all of the booty out here?"

"Damn right I have."

"Check out Gina's."

"Damn."

"Look at Pam's."

"Damn!"

"Even April Reynolds got a fat one!."

"I'll be damned!"

Before I knew it, I was as hard as a bar of gold.

"Yo T, I'm goin' in the water. My jimmy's gettin' hard."

"Mine too."

Now wouldn't that be jacked up to get caught on the bone by the entire senior class! The water was a little cold, but it did the job. When we came out, Tyrone went right back to the grill. He was the fattest Ethiopian I had ever seen! I went over to play volleyball. Only the white kids were playing, but I didn't care. I went to play the game.

"Hi Eric."

"Hi April."

"Wanna play with us?"

"Sure. If you guys don't mind."

"Naw, come on dude!"

I was on April's team. It was April, this other guy named Chip, and me. Real surfer. We played good together. In fact, we were crushin' everybody's team that came over. The *brothers* even came to play. We spanked them too. Then the teachers came. You know we waxed their old butts. Next thing we knew, half the beach surrounded us!

Our class cheered us as we took on these college fraternity guys. Alpha Gamma *something*. They started beating us. You could tell they played all the time. Nonetheless we managed to scratch our way to a tie score for match point. The pressure was on. I had sand all in my *do*. They served. April hit. They spiked. Chip saved. They spiked. I tripped. (Damn!) It went out of bounds. (Whew!) April served. They tried to spike it on me, but I went up for the serious Patrick Ewing rejection! We won! Our whole class went crazy. We shook the loser's hands like a real match and everything.

"Yes!" I exclaimed.

Chip gave me the serious Hi-5. "Killer game bud!"

"Yeah, thanks man."

April jumped on me. "Awesome game man!" "Wanna beer?"

"A what?"

"A beer. Joey Whitmore brought two six packs from his old man's garage."

"Naw, that's alright April, I don't drink."

"You don't?" she asked in amazement.

"No, I don't. You didn't think all black people drank did you?"

I wasn't offended. I just wanted to see where her head was at.

"No man. Not at all. I guess I was just so excited about the game that I just wanted to celebrate. I think. Y'know what I mean right?"

"I understand."

"Thanks." she sighed in relief.

"So what college do you want to go to next year April?"

"My Dad wants me to go to SCU, but I was thinking more like Syracuse University.

"Where's that?"

"Somewhere up in New York."

"New York?" I asked. "Why so far?"

" 'Cause dude, I wanna get away from my family.......and into some new things......y'know, like meet some new people."

"I can dig it." I replied. "Y'know you're pretty cool for a...."

"For a what?" she asked puzzled.

I found myself staring at her thin lips. They looked so different from the ones I'd always seen or even bothered to look at. She was sitting very still.

"Are you nervous Eric?"

"Nervous for what?" I asked.

"Do you wanna kiss?"

I didn't know what to say. So I just kissed her. Slow. It was my first time. Kissing a white girl and all. It was so different. Her, lips, her skin, her hair, her essence. It was kinda nice though.

"Yo man, where you been?" Tyrone asked.

"I ..uh.. had to use the bathroom."

"Yeah right. I saw you walk off with April."

"You did?"

"Yep. Did you get her?" He asked like a little devil. So I played with him.

"Yeah T, we just went and did it behind the water fountain."

"Word up?!?"

"No stupid!"

He was disappointed in me.

"Yo E, you slippin' off bro."

"I'm not even slippin....," I defensively responded. "Besides, have you gotten anywhere with DiSonne yet?"

I just knew he'd get mad. Especially when it came to his dream girl.

"Yo Eric!"

"What."

"Didn't I say I'd get her?"

"Yeah but..."

"Didn't I say I was going to get her?!"

"Yes."

"Alright then!"

"You've got five days left Tyrone."

"I know man."

"120 hours."

"I said I know!"

"Cinco dias."

"Forget you Eric."

I loved messing with my buddy. I knew he had a snowball's chance in hell of even getting a handshake from her. Man, *I* couldn't even mess wit that! Besides, she went out with Sean Wilkens, a big Lee Haney lookin' mub. He was over 6ft. tall like myself. However, he was two hundred and twenty pounds of muscle. I'd still do her fine ass. It'd be worth the risk!

It started getting dark outside so everyone started leaving. Some of the "cooler" students hung out on the beach to get drunk. To hell with that dumb idea! That was something stupid to do. They'd be satisfied when somebody gets killed driving drunk. Or even worse... kills somebody else! I headed straight home. I didn't know why, but for some reason I was horny as hell. It was probably that beach water. Maybe I should've put the move on April. Yeah right. Like I needed a rape trial on my head. Oh well...........

"Hello Monica?"

"Hey babe."

"How are ya?"

"I'm fine sugar. How are you?"

"Oh, alright I guess. I could sure use a hug though." I slyly added.

"Oh you could?"

"Yes Mam."

"Well........my arms have been waiting for you."

I was there before I could remember hanging up the phone! As soon as Monica opened her door, I was on her. My body magnetically locked to hers as I kicked her door shut. ran my fingers through her silky hair. I wanted her so badly. I didn't let up. I couldn't. I was on fire! The fact that she reacted to me with the same fervor made me even hornier! I cupped the crotch of her pants. It felt like molten lava! The next thing I knew, we were doing it on the door. Then we hit the couch, to the carpet, to her bar! Eventually we made it to her bed. After about an hour I was tryin' to come! I was sweating like mad. I didn't even sweat like that when I played basketball! By the time I finished, her entire bed was drenched. I kissed her slowly on those red lips. (As though my show was ending.) Just as I began to speak, she said exactly what I was feeling.

"Thanks Eric, I really needed that."

I didn't know why, but that made me feel dirt cheap. It hurt. It really pissed me off!

"What the hell did that mean Monica?"

"It mean anything honey." She tried to explain.

"The hell it didn't, and don't call me honey!"

She saw I was furious, so she tried to get all intellectual.

"Eric, why are you so enraged sweetheart? I simply expressed my overall impression of your performance."

Of course I couldn't counter that. So I just spoke my mind.

"I wanna go home."

"Do you have to?"She quickly asked.

"No. I just want to."

I jumped up and grabbed my clothes. When I came out of her bathroom, she was leaning on the door with her robe on.

"Eric, I'm so sorry. I never meant you any harm. I sincerely hope you believe that."

I was confused. I didn't know what I believed. I couldn't think. All I knew was that I was disgusted. So I just left.

Chapter 12:

Practical Jokes

SUNDAY AT WORK. THINGS were pretty slow all day. So I had time to play. Me and this guy named John always cracked on each other. He was funny, but I held my own. He told me that my mama was so fat that if she fell out of a tree, she'd go straight to hell! So I told that mob, that his nasty mama was so fat, that if she put on high heels, she could strike oil! We could go for hours. I found out that day that John was a prankster like myself. Needless to say, I found out the hard way. So I'm working the carry-out register. A lot of times my throat would get sore. So I would always pour myself a large orange soda and keep it right beside my register. So business started picking up and I'm taking more orders. Order after order. I was on a roll! (Beep!) I figured let me get a swallow of my good stuff before I took the order. Besides, my last slurp was almost ten minutes ago. So I grab my drink and prepare for the "mega-slurp!" As my lips covered the straw I caught John dying of laughter by the grill. Oh well, I thought gotta get the next order. So I slurped. That fool had put about an inch of salt in the bottom of my cup! I had at least half of it in my mouth. I rushed to the bathroom, drank sink water, and dashed back past a hysterical John to my register. After an entire loaf of hamburger buns and water, I calmly walked over to John. And in my best Bugs Bunny voice…..

"Of course you know……..this means war."

So being the boy-genius that I was, it took no time at all for me to devise a befitting retaliation. I knew that every night at 8o'clock sharp John's wife would call him. Every night he was there. And we had two phones. One in the office, and one by my register. The time was 7:30p.m.. I knew I had to put my devilish plan into action. I was saving my good stuff for a special occasion, but John deserved it. I went over to the sandwich area and grabbed the mayonnaise container. I went over to the phone. Without hesitation, I took a glob of mayonnaise and stuck it on the receiver. It was a lot too. I couldn't wait for him to pick it up! 7:45p.m. John walks outside to get something from his car. I can see him through my window. I would look at him, and then back at the phone. Oh man, hurry up and call lady! 7:55p.m. The phone rings. I fling my window open.

"John, it's your wife man!"

"Thanks bro'!" he yelled back as he dashed inside.

(What a sucker!)

He had his eyes on the ringing phone all the way in. And I had my eyes on him. He never missed his wife's calls. That was real cool. However, he'd <u>never</u> forget this call! My heart was pounding like Christmas time as he neared me. I could feel the wind on all thirty two of my teeth. Just then, plans changed. Dramatically. Just as John got to me, guess who came up behind me? Maurice. (Oh sh-e-e-i-i-t!)

"Y'all don't hear this phone ringing? Damn, I gotta do everything!"

My heart just stopped beating. As I looked into Maurice's face I could see my whole career at Burger King flash in front of me. He spoke............

"Hello?" "Hello?" "I can't hear anyone." "Oh well....."

As he pulled the receiver from his face I saw the goo all over and in his ear! Yuk! He didn't even notice until he hung up the phone. He went off!

"What the hell?"

(Oh snap!)

"Who the.....why would......? **AAARGH!! I'M GONNA KILL ONE OF YOU LITTLE MUTHA----!"**

He stopped because he realized that not only was he screaming, but the entire front line of customers was looking at him. He scanned the whole crew. Menacing as he cleaned his "Helman's head." We were all scared. Even I didn't dare crack a smile in his presence. However, I did need an alibi. So I handed him a damp napkin.

"Here you go Maurice. I can't believe somebody would do something so immature."

He just grabbed the napkin and grumbled back to the office. When the door shut, we all died laughing. I mean, I had laughed in my day, but that day, I almost laughed up a lung!

Chapter 13:

Glory Days

Graduation Day. I woke up at 6:00a.m. sharp. Eventhough the ceremony was at 3p.m., I couldn't go back to sleep. I had been dreaming of me, Monica, Sheila, and Yolana in a pool of whipped cream. Damn, good thing I slept with a rubber on! After my continental breakfast, consisting of cereal, I tried on my cap and gown. While looking in the mirror, I could see myself growing up. Man, I was about to graduate highschool. I think Ma slept with her camera, 'cause soon as she saw me it was like 'click' here, and 'click' there.

"My baby's graduating!" she praised.

I wondered who she told it to most, the neighbors or me. I went to shoot some hoops to shake off some the day's anxiety. Also to escape the loving clutches of Ma. The court up the street was deserted as usual. My jumpshot was hitting. As usual. "Swish. The crowd goes wild! The Lakers have the ball and the Bulls are trailing by 1 point with 10 seconds left on the clock. Oh no, what's this? Michael Jordan has sprained his ankles. Both of them."

"Are you sure you can't play?" The coach asked.

Michael replied, "I'm finished this game coach. Maybe you should put Eric in?"

What? A rookie in Jordan's place? The ball comes into Pippen......9... he brings it up the court....7...he passes to Oakley.....6.....he has it slapped away, but it's recovered by the rookie. (Gotta trade that Oakley guy.) Monroe cuts past Magic.....4....puts the fake on Worthy.....2... and goes for the dunk over Kareem....he's airborne...1..he jams! Oh sweat! I dunked! The crowd lifts me on their shoulders and we all go to celebrate. After the festivities, I give Michael my autograph and head home for my *real* graduation. After I got out of the shower and got dressed, Ma and I ate a special lunch. It was special because she made it especially for me. I ate light because I was already nervous and I didn't need no gas. I left the house at 1:00p.m.. The seniors were suppose to be there no later than 2p.m.. Everyone had on his or her cap & gowns. We looked pretty cool. Our principal, Mr. Stanley, gave us a brief speech about growing up. Then.........we lined up.

I couldn't believe it. It was finally happening. Soon I'd have my diploma in my hands. Just the thought of me not having to break my neck to get to school in the mornings gave me a thrill. When we entered the stadium, the crowd went wild. Everybody's families were there. I was listening out for Ma. Sure enough....

"That's my baby!"

I bet when I turned 50, I would still be her baby. That's cool though. Man, the place was packed! When the last row of seniors filled in, we sat. First, our principal came to the podium.

"Welcome friends, families, and honored guest to this afternoon's celebration of the class of 1989! Now I don't have a long boring speech to say..."

(Thank the Lord.)

"However, I would like to say this. I've known and watched the majority of you grow up. Once you leave this stadium, old Mr. Stanley won't be there to pull you out of trouble. You'll be on your own. You'll have to know what to do, and when to do it. This school's job was to teach you how to do it. You're a special class and I love you all. Good luck and God's speed wherever you go."

After two more speeches, one from our valedictorian, and the other from this man from the Board of Education. Then it was time to present the scholarships and diplomas. They started from the A's and went on down. When they got to the M's, I started shaking. What if I didn't get a scholarship? My entire savings would be spent my first year.

"Donna McClary, a two year scholarship to East Carolina University. Alex Merlo, a four year scholarship to the University of North Carolina-Chapel Hill. Thea Mond, a two year scholarship to Shaw University. Eric Monroe, (Oh Lord please!) a four year scholarship to the University of South Carolina."

I jumped right out of my seat. "Yes!" Ma did the same.

I turned around and she gave me the thumbs up. When I had that diploma and letter in my hand, I felt like a king! The rest of the ceremony was a blur. After everyone received their diplomas, the principal said...

"...All rise. Ladies and gentlemen, I present to you the graduating class of 1989!" We all threw our caps up. Finally. Out in the lobby everyone was hugging and crying. I was so happy. As soon as I got through the doors, there was my Mama. We spread our arms wide.

"My baby boy!"

She was as happy as I was. We cried. After we let go, she told me she would see me back at the house and left with Aunt Jean and Tisha. I saw Tyrone at the other end of the hall with his family. As I walked toward him I heard a familiar voice.

"Hey big boy?"

When I turned, it was who I thought it was.

"Dad!" I yelled.

I ran into his arms without even thinking. He embraced me like I was a baby who just took his first step. The last time I was in his arms, I was about 12. Once I realized what I was doing, I let go. I stuck my hand out for a mature handshake.

"I didn't think you'd come."

"What?" he asked surprised. "And miss my son's graduation?"

As usual, he was with a date. Damn, she couldn't have been much older than I was.

"Oh, son, this is Stacey."

"Hello Stacey."

"So this is the famous Eric." She spoke as though she was impressed by my maturity.

"Yep. That's my boy."

Oh so now all of a sudden he's such a proud father. I decided not to bust his bubble. Besides, Stacey was looking pretty good. Damn, that was screwed up! My no child-support-payin' father shows up at my graduation with a girl half his age and she was checkin' me out!

"Well we gotta get goin'." He smiled as he slipped me $20. "Tell your mama I said hello."

(Yeah, like she'd want to hear that.)

"O.K. Dad. Thanks for coming."

"My pleasure son."

I gave some hugs and some handshakes through the crowd to get to Tyrone.

"Yo 'T'! We did it man!" I yelled.

"Yeah BOEEEY!" He responded.

We jumped straight up for the serious hi-five! Then we hugged.

"Congratulations buddy."

"Ditto Chief."

We were so emotional.

I was huggin' everybody. I hugged all the girls I could. Graduation. The ultimate alibi for a quick feel! When I hugged April, she slipped me a piece of paper and kissed me on the cheek. I didn't know what I was going to do that night, but I had to celebrate.

On my way back home, I put in my Big Daddy Kane tape and cranked the volume all the way! I loved doing that stuff. Especially pulling up the stoplight beside some *old* folk.

I was jammin'! I didn't care who saw me either. Ma had decorated the house with ribbons and posters. She also left a card on the TV. "To my graduating son....". It was a beautiful card. I didn't even notice the money inside. Moms. As I took my gown off, the card April gave me slipped out. It was folded into a little note. Kind of heavy though. When I opened it, there was a key inside. The note said....

"Eric, I enjoyed the beach. For more fun, come to this address at 7o'clock."

There was a business card taped to the key. It must've been her father's 'cause I knew she didn't work at IBM. She didn't even write a number down. I guess she figured I would show up. Like I wanted her little white butt.Shoot... I left the house at 6:30.

The building was downtown, so it was a short drive. I kept looking around for signs of a setup. White folk down south were good for that kind of stuff. If anybody came out, I had my bat. I might've gotten beat up, but damn if I wouldn't go down like Reggie Jackson. Nobody was around, so I went around the back and there she was. She grabbed my wrist.

"C'mon dude!" I followed her. She led me inside to an office.

"Who's office is this?"

"My Father's."She said with a grin.

"Your Father's ?!"

"It's o.k., he won't be back until Monday."

"He better not be."

She sat me down in his chair and knelt between my legs. I knew what was next. She unzipped my fly and began sucking like mad! She kept looking up at me. What? Was I supposed to wave to her or something? Then she completely flipped when she tried to talk dirty to me.

"Oh Eric! I just love the taste of your big...black...manhood in my little white mouth!"

(What the hell?) Damn. I could tell she'd been doing intense research for a dialogue. I wished she would've just stopped, but she kept right on...

"Oh baby, I want you in my tender love box. Give it all to me big daddy!"(Say what?)

I couldn't speak so I thought as loud as I could. (**Girl, would you shut the hell up!**)

When I left that office I had her thinking I was Mandingo!

I never really understood the myth about the black man's penis size. I mean how could somebody know something like that unless you go up to every brother on the street and measure his stuff? Anyway, when I got back home I had to take a quick nap, because I knew I was gonna party all night. When I woke up, I took a shower and started getting ready. The Senior Bash started at 9:00p.m. and ended at 6:00a.m. I couldn't go in that mob alone so I picked up the black book. I didn't see anybody I wanted to take....without doing them. Besides, I was gettin' tired of booty. I just wanted to have a good time. Bingo! Kim.

Yeah, I could take Kim and be safe---and have a great time! I could count on baby sis. Of course she accepted and got the o.k. from Mommy. I picked her up at 8:45 p.m. She came out wearing the dope gear! She looked good. Not as good as me, but close.

"Hey shorty."

"Hey tally."

"Ready?"

"Ready."

"So what's up?" she casually asked.

"Oh nothing much, I just graduated that's all."

"I know that silly. I was just wondering where you been lately. I've been calling you all day."

"Oh well, after graduation, I went and ...uh.... hung out with the fellas for awhile." (Dang, that was close!)

"I hope you're ready to dance girl."

"I'm ready.", she said with the look of a challenge in her eyes. "Jam Jam if you can!"

The place was packed! There were cars lined up on the side of the road. When we got out, we knew we had to hike at least a quarter mile. Halfway there we had to turn and go back to the car. Kim was carrying her purse and I knew she didn't need it.

"...Well, I might need to put some makeup on."

"No you won't. You look just fine, just like you are."

"Thanks man."

There were seniors from all over. I saw some of the fellas.

"Yo what up E!"

"What up?"

"That's your girl man?"

"Naw...I mean...yeah. Yeah she is."

"Yo she look good bro!"

"I know. Now if you gentlemen will excuse us..."

I let Kim pass first so they couldn't look at her butt. Guys.

We went straight to the dancefloor. They were playing "Living on a Prayer" from Bon Jovi. I liked that song. Apparently Kim did too, because she was trying to hang. Then "Groove Me" came on. That was it! I tried to wipe the floor with her, but I couldn't. Every move I made, she countered. She was good. Real good. We stepped off to get some sodas.

"Having a good time?"

"Yeah man!"

I could barely hear her because of the loud music. After about two hours we were both drenched in sweat. So we sat down. The school paid for the catering. Cool! They had all kinds of chips and stuff. Kim wasn't that hungry. I ate like a hog! Hey, it was free. Time had flown. So when midnight approached. I went and called her mother. I told her we were on the way back. She was like, take your time, no rush.

Cool. So we stayed to about 2:30a.m. The place was still rocking! It was dark outside so I held her little hand to the car.

"Where are we going now?" She asked like a little kid.

"I'm taking you home."

"Aw.... man."

"What.... aren't you tired yet?"

"Naw!"

"Well, where do you wanna go then?"

"I don't know."

"Hey I know, let's go to the beach."

"I aint gettin' in no water Eric."

"No duh girl. We can just go walking with our shoes off."

"O.K."

It was a little chilly out there. I guess that was because it was so early in the morning. It was alright though, because we thought ahead and brought jackets. The sand was moist and cool between my toes. The waves rolled lightly onto the shore. It was a pretty romantic scene. I needed one of my women with me.

"Look at your little toes girl."

"What's wrong with them?"

"Nothing. They're cute...just like you."

She smiled.

"Well Eric, your toes are...nice!" She said with a smile.

"Thanks Kim."

"Hey", she jumped, "you wanna race?"

"Girl, you don't wanna........."

By the time I looked, she had taken off! I took off after her. She was fast, but I was gaining on her.

"Here I come girl!"

She tried to pull away with those little "ant" legs, but it was too late. I grabbed her by the waist and lifted her off the sand. A few steps later, we crashed in the sand. We had to crack up.

"You alright?" I asked.

"Yeah."

I rolled over and started brushing the sand off of her face. Her eyes were so big and brown. Like a puppy. I could see the moon in them.

I didn't even give it a second thought. I kissed her. It was like Monica had kissed me. Slow and sweet.

"Wow! What was that for?"

"That was for being you."

"Can I have another one?"

"Of course."

I began caressing her. Rubbing all over her small frame. I knew what was happening. I wanted to stop...but I couldn't. At that I jumped to my feet.

"I...I can't do this Kim."

"Why not?"

"Because."

"Because what? Because I'm too young right?"

"No."

"Then why not Eric?!"

She sounded grown. Almost like Sheila.

"Because...well...I thought you were a virgin."

"Well I'm not."

She was lying. So was I. I would've done it with anyone else, but not Kim. She's special. She's different than rest. Before I could say let's go home, she was back in my arms.

She placed her hands inside my jacket and pressed her head into my stomach. I hugged her back. In a sympathetic way. That only made things worse. Since I had already unbuttoned her shirt, there wasn't much left on her. I reached to button it back and she unzipped her shorts. She was ready. I felt dizzy. Everytime I looked at her, she looked older. She looked.... sexier.

(This isn't right. **Take her.** No. **Take her damn it!** No, she's just a kid! **Does her body look like a kid's to you?** No. **Then do it.** I can't. **Yes you can!** No!! I said no and that's final! **You soft ass punk! It's right there in front of you!** I know. **Then do it fool. You like her don't you?** I love her. **Then fuck her.**)

And I did.

As I laid down on top of her little body, I noticed that her fists were clenched. As though preparing for a struggle. I parted her legs and began entering her. She was definitely a virgin. She cringed at the point of contact. I didn't want to hurt her, but it was like trying to fit a bowling ball in a marble bag. Still I forced myself inside of her. She just laid there courageously as I took her innocence from her. I wanted to get it over with. I could hear her gasping with each stroke. When it was over, I went to kiss her like I did everyone else. I saw a tear running down the side of her face. She quickly wiped it off. It broke my heart. If I even had one. I drove her home without a word. She kissed me goodnight, but I couldn't feel it. I was numb. I had just violated my best friend in the whole world. Maybe my Dad was right when he once told me, "Boy....you ain't shit."

Chapter 14:

A Different World

THE UNIVERSITY OF SOUTH Carolina. First semester was going fairly easy. I got so many numbers! There were so many students. Just like on TV. It was like a whole different planet. I liked it though. When I left home for college, nobody but Ma knew. I snuck out on the down low. Besides, I didn't want to deal with anybody. That summer was just horrible. I just wanted it over so I could get out of there. I had to put in crazy hours at work to save up. Which meant Sheila would have crazy opportunities to get in my face. Some people just don't know when to stop. One day her boyfriend came to the store, and she told him to wait in the dining room. Then, she rushed over to me and took me to in the office. That girl put my hand inside her panties! Then went right back up to the front like nothing. Needless to say I was scared as hell! Mike even looked over at me! I threw up the peace sign with the quickness. For more reasons than one! I went bowling with Tisha and Yolana. We ran into a couple of their classmates. Some little guys acting like toughguys. Kids. Nah, they were cool. We played pool and everything. I kinda dug the little guys. That is until we went to the bathroom and one of them told me he was doing Yolana.

"Excuse me?"

"Yeah, boy! She got a nice one. I was on it yesterday."

I had to be as calm as possible while this fool babbled on.

"So you guys are doin' it?"

"Oh yeah, troop, I been in that booty for a couple of weeks now."

"Word up?"

"Word. I'ma get some today too!"

"Knock it out bro!", I said as I gave him five. Half of me wanted to knock this little punk out. I could feel the truth in his words. It cut like a knife. When we came out, I avoided every attempt of contact from Yolana. Even when she tried to graze by me I slid over. She didn't understand. I knew it when I looked into her eyes. My Mama taught me how to tell if somebody is lying. I don't know what pissed me off worse. The fact that Yolana was cheating on me, or that I couldn't say or do anything about it. Fine, I thought. Who needed her anyway. I felt so betrayed.

Monica invited me over and cooked me a meal that turned out to be my farewell dinner. Right in the middle of my salad she told me she was getting married. She was so cool about it. I mean, what could I say? I just asked her if the guy made her happy. She started talking about his job and all. We made love one last time and I left. I wished her happiness. Although, I knew it would be hard for her to find. I learned a lot from that lady. Maybe too much.

After a few weeks, I dropped my Psychology class. It was too boring. Besides, this girl I had sexed was in there and she was psycho! She kept looking at me all starry-like. Freaked me out. I needed another course to complete my credit standards. So I picked up Creative Writing. Which I knew nothing about. I bugged out my first day there. It was females galore in that mob! (Yeah buddy!) I was scopin' all of 'em. Trying to look and sound as intelligent as possible. Our professor was a playwright that had taught at Harvard. I was impressed. Shame he was gay. I just couldn't get with that. I mean, that was his business and all, but not for the kid. I mean … he was cool. I just wasn't taking no chances. Something very interesting did catch my eye though. There was this girl in the corner of the classroom with all these buttons on her jacket and hat. They were all different colors. She looked like a bag of skittles! She stuck out like a sore thumb. I mean compared to the rest of the student body, she dressed corny. She was kinda cute though. I wanted to talk to her. Oh what the heck, I thought. Maybe I could get some of that "cornball" booty. After class, I stepped to her.

"Excuse me sister?"

"Yes?" She responded in delight.

I tried to drop one of my famous lines on her.

"You have pretty eyes."

That line normally cracks the ice and goes straight to their heads, but it didn't work on her.

"Is that so?", she said emotionlessly.

There was a pause. I didn't know what to say. I felt so uncomfortable. I had to say something.

"Hey.... I'm not trying to come on to you or anything like that...."

"Well, that's good." She spoke with a gentle smile.

I couldn't figure her out. It was like I was being dissed very nicely. Well, I wasn't about to go out like that. Especially not by a nerd. I swallowed my embarrassment and extended my hand.

"My name is Eric."

"Hello Eric, my name is Lynn."

"So, Lynn, what interested you in taking this writing class?" Well I couldn't think of anything else to say.

"I took Creative Writing because it allows me to express myself through literature. Know what I mean?"

"Uh-yeah."

She smiled.

"Why did you join Eric?"

"I just wanted to drop Psyche', so I picked up this one."

"Why did you do that?"

"Because this girl, I-I mean I wasn't satisfied with the course."

"Well did you confront your Prof.?"

I wanted to change the subject. Quickly.

"It's no big deal Lynn."

"I see."

There was something weird about this girl. Something I liked, yet hated at the same time. I didn't quite know what to say next so I did the inevitable.

"Uh... Lynn, would you like to have lunch?"

"Why sure, that would be great Eric." she said with little enthusiasm.

So we went to a little cuisine I regularly visited called "Che' McDonald's." We ate for awhile without speaking. I kept avoiding her eyes. I didn't want to stare at her. Besides she was looking dead in my face!

"So, Eric, tell me about yourself."

Oh sweat! I wondered what that meant!

"Well, there's really not much to tell. I like music, girls, TV, sports. Y'know typical guy stuff. What about you?"

"Well I like music also."

"Really. What kind?"

"Gospel."

"Oh."

"What do you mean oh?"

"I didn't mean anything. It's just that that's kinda weird."

"Weird?"

I didn't know how or why, but I was diggin' myself deeper and deeper in the hole.

"Well-yeah, weird. I mean yo, here you are a young fly girl like yourself and you're into gospel. Don't you like Rap music?"

"Not particularly."

"How about R&B? I know you like New Edition. Bobby Brown?"

She didn't blink.

"No Eric, I don't prefer that type of music."

Now I was offended!

"And why not?"

"Because that type of music is not what I'm about. It's secular. They sing about violence, drugs, and pre-marital sex. All of which, I don't believe in, stand for, or agree with. So why should I be into that?"

(Damn!)

My mouth was wide open in shock. I couldn't believe she just said that.

"I can't believe you just said that."

"Why not Eric?"

"Well...I don't know, it just seems like you're judging me or something!"

"I'm not here to judge you brother."

"Then why are you here?" I snapped.

"You asked me to lunch remember?"

"Fine. Then let's have lunch!"

"Are you alright?" She asked so sweetly.

"Wait a second Lynn, I think we're getting off on the wrong foot here. I'm sorry."

"Oh it's alright. Perhaps your conscience needs to be cleared."

"Say what?"

"Or perhaps your spirit is burdened?"

"Hey...what'chu talkin' 'bout girl?"

She smiled as though she knew I was going to say that. Then it came out.

"Eric, I'm talking about a different lifestyle. I'm talking about a relationship with God."

"Oh yeah?" I interjected as a matter of fact like. "Well I believe in God."

"You do?"

"Yes I do."

"What do you believe about him?"

"First of all, I was raised in the church, o.k.?"

"That's great Eric, but that's not what I asked you."

"My Mother is even on the Church Board of Trustees...."

"That's nice too but......."

"Alright Lynn, I believe that God is the Supreme Being of the earth! Are you satisfied?"

"And?"

"And that he loves me. I know the whole scenario Lynn."

"Do you know who Jesus Christ is?" She persisted.

"Of course I know who Jesus was!"

"That's not what I asked you."

"Yes it was!"

"No sir, it wasn't. I asked you if you know who Jesus <u>is</u>.

By this point, I saw I couldn't debate with her. And I didn't want to be childish and leave.

"No Lynn, tell me."

"Eric, Jesus was, is and always will be the Son of God. He came down from heaven to die for our sins. Yours and mine. He did it because he loves us. And all he asks us in return is our lives for his service. When I heard about Jesus, I wasn't sure either, but I prayed in faith that if he was real, for him to come into my heart and make me over into what he needs me to be. Y'see heaven and hell are very real. And I know now that if and when I die, my soul belongs to God. Not because he made me, but because I gave my life to him. The world is full of sin and perversion. However, the Bible teaches us that the wages of sin is death, but the gift of God is eternal life. Do you believe that Jesus can heal you Eric?"

"Heal me? I ain't sick!"

"I didn't think I was either brother."

This girl was a trip. She had me mesmerized. The average person giving me a sermon like that would have been talking alone by then. But I couldn't get mad at her. She sounded so very sweet. She seemed like a little girl defending her daddy. I found myself staring into her face.

"You really believe all that Lynn?"

"As sure as the air I breathe."

"Can I ask you a personal question?"

"Sure you can."

"Are you like-well-you-know..."

"What?"

"Are you like-um... having sex?"

"No Eric, I'm not."

"Do you ever think about it?"

"No."

"C'mon."

"No, I don't. Why should I?"

"Haven't you ever seen a real good looking guy and thought about it."

"Sometimes I wonder what it will be like on my honeymoon with my husband."

"That's it?"

"Yes sir. Y'see Eric, a clean heart keeps a clean mind, which keeps a clean mouth, and promotes a clean lifestyle."

"So why are you telling me all of this Lynn?"

"Because Jesus loves you Eric."

"I know that Lynn."

"Then why don't you love him back? Let him into your life Eric."

After that day, I did all I could to avoid Lynn. I would take opposite routes to classes and everything. I didn't know if I was afraid or angry. How could she talk to me like that? She didn't know me. She didn't know anything about me. Something was wrong though. Something was gnawing at me from the inside. The only thing I was sure about was that I was confused. I couldn't think straight. It got worse everyday.

I talked to Ma and she not only agreed with Lynn, but she fell in love with her and begged to meet her. Eventually, I ran into Lynn.

"Hi."

"Hello."

"Listen, I've been thinking about what you said."

"That's great." She smiled.

"Well, it's like this...since that day we had lunch I haven't had much rest. Y'know?"

"I see."

"You didn't put the whammy on me did you?"

"The whammy?"

"Nevermind I just feel so weird."

"Maybe God is trying to tell you something."

(Now where have I heard that before?)

That following Sunday, I went to church with Ma as usual. The preacher was going off as usual, and the congregation was going off! As usual. After yet another rousing sermon, came the invitation. I'd heard invitations most of my life, but the one I was about to hear changed my life. He said;

"Family, Jesus loves us. He loves us so much that he gave his life not only for us, but also for our sins. And he's still inviting us to let him inside. Inside our heart and lives. I challenge you to get to know Jesus. Why don't you come to him? I believe the Spirit of God is calling someone here. Somebody here is sick. Somebody's sick and don't know they're sick. Somebody here is lonely. I say someone here is in the need of prayer! Oh, I pray you don't leave today without Him. Tomorrow is not promised to any man. God loved us enough to give us a second chance. Don't turn away."

At that moment, I realized that I had been living wrong. All those women. All of that sex. I felt so guilty. So filthy. I heard a still small voice...

"Come home."

I lifted my head to look at Ma. I started crying. My head was swimming. I couldn't concentrate on anything but going down the aisle to the altar. So I stood up, knees shaking and everything. I knew I had to make a change. I had to!

"Then I heard the other voice. The same voice I heard when I took Kim's virginity.

"Yo, what'chu doin'?"

"I'm going to the altar."

"Man.......sit your ass down!"

"I-I can't."

"Of course you can. Now hurry up before somebody sees your dumb ass!"

I began sitting.

"Come home son."

I stood back up. This time I took a step.

"Hey man, you can't go down there!"

"Why not?"

"Because that's for Christians. You aint no *real* Christian!"

"I don't care. I'm going."

"Don't go!" The voice persisted. **"I can get you those women back."**

"I don't want them."

"How about some new ones?"

"No!"

"Any women?!"

"No!!!"

"Alright then…what about Lynn?"

Halfway to the altar I stopped.

"What about her?"

"Oh come on Eric, you know you want her."

"No I don't."

"Liar! You were thinking about her naked at lunch. You can't fool me."

"Well…I was wrong."

"No you weren't, you were being human. Hey, I bet her nipples get hard."

"Stop it! Don't talk about her!"

"I bet you wish you could lick'em don't you?"

"She's not like that!"

"Oh but you are."

"Stop it!!"

"Y'know she get's wet when she thinks about you don't you?"
"Shut up!"
"Just imagine her tongue on you...."
"Damn you!!!!!"
"NO, DAMN *YOU*!! HA! HA! HA! HA!"
I was literally crawling. My chest was tight. My heart felt like a time-bomb. I was convulsing. But nobody cared. Nobody tried to help me. They just stared at me. I felt like my life was slipping from me. As though a part of me, a huge part of me....was dying. When I finally got to the altar, the Preacher simply asked, "Son, why are you here?"

And without doubt or hesitation I uttered, "I surrender."

Chapter 15:

New Life

THAT DAY THE OLD Eric died and the new Eric was born again. I had a new walk and a new talk! I began fellowshipping with Lynn. I finally opened the Bible bought me years before. It had so much dust on it, I mistook its real blue cover for gray! Shame. I began learning what real love was about. I also fell in love with Lynn. It was holy love. I had never felt that type of affection except from Ma. I had begun a new life and I was in love for the first time in my life. Life was great!

Lynn and I started dating. We would go to prayer meetings. This was totally different from my dates in the past. With us, there was no kissing on the lips. No isolation from society. It was like we were little kids again. It was cool though, that was to help us avoid temptation. The Bible taught us that if we resisted the devil, then he would flee from us. Oh, I was getting good! We went ice skating, where I busted my bottom repeatedly! Everything was perfect…until I got sick. It started out as a sore throat, then a cold that just wouldn't go away. Then, I started dropping weight. I couldn't keep much food down. And I got tired alot. I ignored it as long as I could. Soon afterwards while at the park with Lynn, I coughed up blood. Test after test. X-ray after x-ray. Having to eat hospital food for a week. Finally, the doctors told me that I had been infected with the AIDS virus. Because of the fact that I took no precautions or prevention, my condition would only worsen.

Everything came apart at the seams. I had to drop out of school. It wasn't that I was ashamed, it was just nobody's damn business! I moved back home. I hated to tell Ma.

"Mama?"

"Yeah baby?"

"I'm sick."

No more words were necessary. She cried. All night long. I could hear her from my room late at night.

"Oh Lord God, please don't take my baby from me. Please Lord, take me."

Lynn called and said she wanted to see me. I had run out of excuses and finally decided to face her. Since the last time she saw me I had lost close to 20lbs.When I opened the door, the expression on her face said it all.

"Eric? What happened to you?"

"I'm sick Lynn."

"What's wrong?"

"I have a virus."

She stared at me from top to bottom in disbelief.

"Oh God, Eric, how could this have happened? You don't use any drugs do you?"

"No I don't." I didn't think she would understand. I withdrew. "Nevermind Lynn, I'll be fine."

"Eric. Talk to me. I want to help you."

"You can't help me with this."

"Why not?"

"Because---I--" I knew I loved her. I knew I had to tell her. "Lynn, I think I love you."

"I love you too Eric..." She smiled in relief.

"Please let me finish. I've been through a whole lot in the past few years. I've been with a whole lot of different people…in relationships and stuff. I was having...sex." I was so embarrassed that I couldn't even look into her face. I fornicated. I thought that I knew what love was, but I didn't. Not until I met you. I thought that having sex was the best way to show someone that they meant something to you. I never knew how wrong I was until right this moment. You have shown me that love really is patient, and it really is kind. I know now that if you really love someone, you don't think like that about them. You think about making them happy and spending time with them. You sacrifice for them. You care. Since I accepted Jesus as my savior, He's taught me. He's taught me that love is like a tree. It has to be rooted in a firm foundation. You have to give it alot of attention. You have to respect it. And if you continue to love and cherish it, one day it will not only take care of itself, but it can also take care of you." She was speechless. "God knows that you bring me joy Lynn, and all I want to do is make you as happy as you deserve to be for as long as I can. I want to someday marry you and maybe raise a family with you. But.... that cannot be."

"What do you mean?" she whispered in fear.

"What I mean is......I'm dying. I'm dying of AIDS."

I felt like a ton was lifted from my shoulders. Yet I still couldn't manage to look up in her face. I knew I had to. She stared at me. A small tear streamed down her face. And without another word, we hugged. I felt like a kid again in my Mama's arms.

When Lynn left, I was so full of emotion I ran in my room and collapsed on my bed. I stuffed my pillow as far in my mouth as I could and screamed at the top of my lungs. I cried myself to sleep. I dreamt a dream. I saw myself at age 5 again. Sitting in my room on the floor with my Lego's. I heard the door crack open. I turned only to see my Mama standing there with the proudest smile on her face. Her expression meant the world to me. I knew I was good. She spoke to me.

"What are doing down there baby boy?"

With glee I jumped to my feet and pointed at my creation and said, "I'm buildin' you a house Mama!"

And then I was awakened.

"Sh-h-h baby", she said. "Mama's got you. Everything's alright now. Mama's here."

I couldn't see her. I could only hear her. She was kissing my face. Mama. As big as I was, in her lap. Funny thing though, it didn't feel wrong. I felt relaxed. At peace. Finally free.

That night, Eric Monroe died in his sleep. Just two weeks before his 19th birthday. He lost a short battle with a full blown AIDS virus. A foe he never saw coming. A promising, young, intelligent black man... gone.

At his funeral his Mother sat staring aimlessly into nothingness. Countless family and friends tried to console her, but she felt nothing.

Nothing but the unimaginable void of her child's presence. His smile. Miss Tishana Franklin, his favorite cousin, gave the eulogy.

"Eric was a beautiful bright young man. I loved him with all of my heart. He was always so sweet. He could always make me laugh. My cousin. I can't believe you're gone. I still see your face every day. When we were kids we went through everything. From breaking each other's toys to playing in the bathtub. From climbing trees to getting caught in the closet. Eric could always talk me into trouble, but with that smile of his he could always get me out. We always did ...." She couldn't finish. She had to be helped from the floor.

Mr. Tyrone Jarrett,

Eric's best friend hadn't seen him since highschool graduation. Still, he was always there for his friend. A few others showed. Needless to say, most of his "female associates" were there. Among them were Monica, who had gotten married one year prior. She brought her two year old son, Erin. Sheila, who broke off her engagement to Mike when she caught him in their bed with another................... **man!**

Yolana, who ran away from home only to join the Nation of Islam, came to pay her respects. She had vowed a life of celibacy until the right "brother" came along. Kim wasn't there. She reportedly was strung out on crack cocaine and was sentenced to five years in prison for attempting to sell her baby to an undercover police officer.

If only Eric had known. If only he had learned. If only there was such thing as a "do-over" life. He would've known how much he was adored. Not for his body or any material, but for the treasure inside of him. Outside was a bright young man with a promising future who happened to be exceptionally charming for his age. Inside he was a sweet little boy. A little boy whose love was misled, misguided if you will, into the false realm of a "man's world."

A world for which he was neither mentally nor spiritually prepared for. You see, no one ever spoke to him about sex. He only knew what his father showed him in pornography. His mother refused to see or even acknowledge the reality of it. She saw what she wanted to see of her son. With the pressures of sex in society, on television, in music, and even in the magazines, Eric, like most children, are misguided into their views of love and commitment. He thought that in order to be a man, you had to do it. And you had to do it with a lot of women. And now.... he's dead. His father didn't even come to his funeral.

In the wake of Eric Monroe, I am compelled to testify. Though he is gone his story is very much alive and in our communities. It is alive in our families, our children, and even our children's children. Race, gender, economics, or background. The disease of lust and immoral sex has plagued the world for centuries. It continues to do so even in our homes today. We tend to overlook or confuse it until disaster strikes. Disaster often goes hand in hand with ignorance. Ignorance is exemplified when you don't know the truth and you decide to make it right by your own standards and then call it truth. Or you just don't care at all. We cannot continue to live this way. In the end, not only do we suffer, but so do our children. There are millions of fatherless children. Mothers are abandoning or even selling their babies. Rape cases in high schools across the country. Rape in the family. Rape at work. Child molestation. Dear God, the list seems infinite!

Imagine the cases that will never be reported. How many dreams are lost? How many artists, leaders, and geniuses have we lost because of misguided love? The Bible says, "The sins of the people will fall upon the children..." Contrary to the ideas of the world, we are not created to be sexual creatures. We are from God Almighty. He is LOVE; therefore, we are creatures of love. However, that love must be restrained, groomed, and guided, and prepared until the time it can fully blossom in beauty.

Lovemaking, not sex, was designed by God specifically for the enhancement, pleasure and unity of a man and woman bound and intertwined in the security of marriage and commitment. Even though times have changed, there are old fashioned principles that remain the same. Sex without commitment is a death trap. Our children are in a world that has all but lost these values. They deal with these issues and more at unthinkable ages. They are not exempt at school, in the community, or in some cases, even at home! They are being misled into thinking that they can use their bodies immorally with no consequence. Teen pregnancy, rape, incest and molestation and such crimes continue to scar our babies. The effects can plague them for their entire lives. Then the cycle continues. All because of hurt people who continue to hurt people. We who know this have to arm ourselves and protect the innocent. Regardless of who you are, death and disease won't ask you your name. They will only devour you. I believe that along with faith, education is a priceless tool to use to protect us. We have to fight. We have to take a stand for the innocent. It is a never ending battle. But it's like my Mama always said, "Do your best baby, and God will take care of the rest."

Thank you Jesus. Thank you for your blood and your Holy Spirit. Through your love and guidance, I know now that Eric had to die......... so that I could live.

I encourage you. Be strong. Love yourselves. Respect yourselves for the beautiful creatures that you are. Teach this invaluable lesson to your children. Guide them.

For misguided love will always fail.

The End.

Epilogue

Eric

I don't know where I went wrong. I mean I heard about sex and everything, but I just couldn't control myself! I was just like a bee that got his first taste of honey. I went crazy! Everywhere I went and everything I did was somehow linked to sex. I looked at every pair of legs that passed my eyes. Every pair was a possibility. I was even watchin' 11 and 12 year olds! By my first semester in college, I had screwed over twenty different girls. I didn't even know half of their names. I didn't really give a damn either.....until I got inside that is. The more I got it, the more I wanted it. I didn't think I had no problem though. It wasn't like money or drugs. It was just some sex. Right?

Yolana was cool. She had a cute booty too. She just wasn't my type. She was cool for doin' the nasty and all, but that was about it. We never went anywhere. Probably because I didn't feel like listening to her "hair-brained" lingo! Just ditsy! After a month or so, her "perky" attitude annoyed the crap out of me.

I tried insulting her one day by saying, "You know Yolana, sometimes I wish my I.Q. was lower, that way I could better enjoy your company!" That line went right over her head. She thought she was so slick. Always had an excuse for something. Always somewhere opposite of where she was supposed to be. Then be the first one to flash that big ole "Chucky Cheese" grin in your face. I wouldn't trust her with a ball of lint! She was probably doing other guys while I was with her. Oh well.

Sheila? She got on my last nerve. Don't get me wrong, she had the dope body and all, but damn. She treated me like I was a stray dog. After being with her, I got a craving for milkbones! I never understood what she needed me for. If she was that unhappy with Mike, then why didn't she just break up with him? She probably wanted to dog him like he was probably doggin' her. And I was the perfect tool. She wanted to have her cake and <u>do it</u> too! She wasn't straight with me, so I couldn't be honest with her. I'd still screw her though.

Monica. Monica. Monica. Man, now that was a woman! She was special. I learned alot from her. She was almost like a big sister. Except that she had the most gorgeous face in the world! I liked being with her. I knew she knew I was a teenager, but she acted like it wasn't even an issue, so I did the same. She taught me how to be patient in bed. How to take it one step at a time...each time you do it. She was suave. Very intelligent. But with all of that success, smarts, and beauty going for her, she found herself in bed with a 17 year old kid. I wanted to be the man that she wanted, but I knew I couldn't. Maybe she'd find "Mr. Right" one day. Or maybe she'd have to settle for "Mr. could be." I miss her, with her fine self.

Kim. Kimmy was my buddy. My homegirl. My main squeeze. My baby sis'. My partner in crime. My little smurfette. My best friend. And I lost her. And I'm the one to blame. I had her as the friend I needed, and I blew it. I never should have done it. I knew how she looked up to me...and I used her. She was so special to me. God knows she was. I just had no other way of expressing my feelings for her. I thought it would be alright if we did it, but everything changed. Everything. She started calling me all the time. Everyday! At least ten times a day! She started trying to dress like she was grown or something. It made her look cheap. She started cursing and hanging out. She even had the nerve to offer me a cigarette one day! I felt like cramming the whole pack down her throat. But I couldn't. This was my fault. Daily I would think, "Look what I did to her." She lost her innocence. Her sparkle. Her glow. It got to the point where I couldn't stand the sight of her. It hurt too much. So I just left town without good-byes. I wish I could've done it over with. I'd treat her right. I wish I could talk to her. I miss her.

Maybe the Pastor at church was right about not abusing our sexuality. And about enjoying my youth and stuff. I should've listened. He was right all the time. But it's too late now. I'm way past that now. My life was so very special. I learned too late. All of those women. All of that sex. They didn't love me. How could they have? I didn't even love myself! They probably won't even remember me. If they do it will be as a whore or some kinda gigolo. Oh God! Why me? Why did you let me die? Am I responsible for my own wrongs? I didn't know any better! I can't even cry. I am frozen, but I can't even feel the cold.

I remember watching my Grandfather when I was a child. He would always pick flowers for Grandma. One day, he picked this really pretty rose. He cut it at the stem with his Swiss-army knife.

"Granddaddy?" I questioned as I tugged at his big pocket. "That flower is gonna die now aint it?"

He smiled down at me. "Sure it will son, but when you give it with your heart and not your hand, it can last forever."

I clearly didn't understand that one. He knew it too.

"Don't worry son, you'll get it someday."

Granddad gave Grandma flowers every Sunday morning. For years I heard. Even up until the day he died. I was twelve years old. Grandma would be out in her garden every Sunday after that. They loved each other. Wholeheartedly. That kind of love can't be bought. It can't be sold. Nor can it be portrayed. It's the kind of love that I never knew for myself. It was patient and kind...

I wish I could've loved like that. I wish.

Yolana

Eric? Eric was a trip. From the moment I laid eyes on'em I wanted him. He was cool. He knew just what to say. That boy could get me wet at the drop of a hat. Whew! I didn't need no boyfriend and I guess he felt the same. We never really said that to each other. I guess it was just understood. The sex was amazing! He was thick. I could barely close my hand around that thing! Out of all the guys I was having sex with, Eric was the best. That was messed up. He was faithful to me all the while I was screwin' around. Well, the last guy I fell for did that to me. So I promised myself that that would never happen to me again. Shi-i-i-t! I had to get mine! Now that he's gone, I don't do it as much as I used to. Basically, now because I'm "righteous." I've been reading the Qu'ran. Besides all of that, some fool gave me gonorrhea! Nonetheless, it is alright. Allah will heal me. I miss Eric though, with his sexy self.

Sheila

I liked Eric. Not just because he was good looking, but also because he knew how to say the right things. Damn, he was charming! So full of energy. He knew how to make me feel like a woman. I didn't care how old he was. And since Mike was messing up I needed a break. I felt like an old tired lady with him. Eric made like a kid again. Like taking risks and stuff. I figured it like this, he wouldn't complain about Mike since he was gettin' some older booty. It was going fine until he started lying. Damn it! I hate that. Why do men have to do that? Never satisfied. Giv'em some money, they spend it on other women. Giv'em some sex, they screw other women. Giv'em an inch, and they'll run a marathon on you! That's why you gotta watch them. Carefully. I knew Eric probably had a little girlfriend, but he had to learn how to be faithful. I feel bad though. He was so promising. I dream about him all the time. That's the only way I can still sleep with him.

I want him back.

Monica

Eric was a six-foot tall chocolate dreamboat, with a smile that could charm the panties off a Nun. Eric was indeed special. I would've never even considered dating anyone his age, but his smile and charisma were irresistible. That was definitely no teenager! I was drawn to him. I could bask in him for days. He had the maturity of a thirty-year-old. Yet he had the vivacity of a five-year-old. He respected me. He treated me like a woman should be treated. His mother raised him well. I loved the way he tried so hard to do things right. He wasn't afraid to make mistakes. He was always there when I needed him. I only wished him older. I'd propose to *him*. I could've fallen in love with that kid. I tried to remind myself of that when I was without him. However, when I was with him, the irrelevance was astounding! I wanted him. He had his entire future in front of him though. I knew that I couldn't be the part of that. I'm grateful for the opportunity to be with him for the short time that it was. I've dated many men much older than him, but there was something about him that transcended him far beyond the rest. Perhaps a man's problems stem from within himself. Like when he refuses to acknowledge vulnerability. I loved that about Eric. He knew that he wasn't perfect, but he tried. For a kid, Eric was one hell of a man!

Kim

I loved Eric. He was my knight in shining armor. I wanted to be everywhere he was. He was like the perfect big brother. Only I had a crush on him. He looked at me like I was special. He didn't treat Cyndi like he treated me. She was so jealous. 'Cause every time she saw him, she always had something bad to say. After we did it that night, I was constantly be in her face. She stopped speaking to me for a long time. She just mad because she's probably **still** a virgin! I thought that Eric would like her instead of me, but I'm so glad he didn't. I wish I had his address at school. I need to talk to him. He probably wouldn't even recognize me now. I've got so many things to tell him. I just got out of the Southern Youth Correctional Center. I've grown an inch taller. I cut my hair down. I'm gettin' ready for the 11th grade this year. I'm HIV positive. *And* that we have a son named E.J. Soon as I save up enough, I'll find him. He'll want to be with me now. I just know he will!